Chapter 1: Prayer in the

The Praying Church

The Praying Church
with study guide

Donald M. Hultstrand

A Crossroad Book
The Seabury Press · New York

1977
The Seabury Press
815 Second Avenue
New York, N.Y. 10017

Printed in the United States of America

Library of Congress Cataloging in Publication Data

Hultstrand, Donald M   1927-
   The praying church.
   1.Prayer. I.Title.
BV210.2H83   248'.3   77–8337
ISBN 0–8164–2159–5 pbk.

Contents

Preface

A book entitled *The Praying Church* might be misconstrued from the beginning. There are those who, through habit of mind, would immediately assume it had to do with worship. That it does, but only in part. We are dealing here with the Church in the broadest sense, the Church as the Body of Christ.

This is a Church that is sometimes gathered for worship. More often it is found in small groups—organizations, families, commissions, task forces, and prayer groups. Always it is manifested as the Church Scattered, a reference to our lives as they are lived out on the plane of daily life.

This book is not intended as a volume for scholars. It hopes to deal practically with matters of Christian living. Much of it, therefore, is experiential. How can a writer express what prayer means for the meeting of daily demands of the world, and what he understands as the will of God, except through what he has experienced? Quickly, one may say, "It can be expressed through the experiences of others." This is true, and there will be ample examples of this. But when all is said and done, even the most touching experiences of others will neither be discovered nor appreciated unless they somehow have a meeting place in the experience of the writer.

Why do I make this effort to write of the Praying Church? Is there any other kind of Church? I think not. Yet this is precisely the point. There have been many who have been able to describe the Church, work for the Church, and consider its task without speaking of prayer. It was as if they were dealing with an organization which had membership, business, survival techniques, and teachings (always under question), but in which piety was eccentric. Either it was the chosen lot of a few zealots who were suspected of unearthly escapism, or it was honored by hymnology and liturgy, which were seldom thought of as prayer but as parts of an observance.

Sadly, this left the Church in a desert of humanism. The very quest for relevance in education and social concern led to even further dryness and irrelevance. The guilt and frustration of those who attempted to deal with God's world without turning consciously to Him caused many to give up with the worldly cynicism which is often the other side of the coin of worldly idealism. The ideals were devoid of life and so, for many, they became frustrating idols.

What we speak of here, then, is a churchmanship in which God and man are constantly and consciously in communication. It is prayer on a continuing basis, which evades neither God nor the world He has made. It is built upon a frank acknowledgment that prayer is the central issue of our time. Either we are the people of God, the Body of Christ, or we aren't. We insist that we are, and if so, we cannot possibly know Him too well or deal with Him too much. Thus, in the Praying Church, we discover that the central work is always the inculcation of the spiritual life.

In deep gratitude for the Easter people, who have demonstrated to me that Christ still lives in their midst, I set forth these words, each of which came out of imperfect prayer.

1 Prayer in the Gathered Church

To be a member of the Body of Christ, the Church, is to be a person of prayer. This is a simple statement, but its ramifications are as complex as the totality of life. We are speaking of a prayer life that is active on every plane of our existence.

First of all, consider prayer in the Gathered Church. We call it worship. It is the body of Christ coming together to adore the Triune Lord. It could easily be said to be the Great Prayer. We encounter people who rarely think of worship as "prayer." Prayers are acknowledged as part of its framework but there is an undefined, unexpressed feeling that the whole experience is that of attending a "religious program."

From the least structured free churches to the most formalized liturgical churches there are elements that are recognizable from the secular world of programming: speeches, songs, education, readings, solo presentations, and group presentations. There is even that portion which is like a "commercial," when "advertisements" for meetings, bake sales, bazaars, and educational programs are heralded.

To consider the whole of worship as prayer becomes a matter for concentration and commitment. It makes a great deal of difference whether people come there with a conscious spirit of adoration or, vaguely, to be a warm body at a religious program. Where worship meets its intention, to express the worth-ship of a God who creates, redeems, and sanctifies, it is more than words. Great liturgy cannot express adequately that which is more than itself. On the other hand, free forms of worship need to acknowledge the same inadequacy.

What is happening in worship is an encounter of God with His gathered flock. Let us suppose that someone who is essentially a stranger to the Church begins to walk past the entrance as he goes along the sidewalk. He feels drawn to go in. He has come to a point of realization that there must be more to life than he has found. He walks timidly into the church, for the service is already in process. People like himself are there. What brings them here? What seizes them? As he stands at the back of the aisle he senses that the very air is different, charged with a Presence. There is something happening here which passes understanding. Here, somehow, is the very gateway of heaven.

An idealistic dream? It may sound as such to some, but it is the very experience reported by persons who have entered a church where worship has become a total act of prayer. To expect less is to underestimate the dimensions of that which is actually taking place. The God of eternity is meeting with His people in a particular atmosphere of praise and expectation.

If this is so, then we are to expect great things to happen in such an encounter: conversions, reconciliations, healings, inspirations, commitments, and commissions. We have usually been guilty of expecting too little of worship rather than expecting too much. This is not to detract from the "pureness" of worship, which is to insist that it is for the glorification of God and not for the fulfillment of our needs. It is, rather, to celebrate His presence in such a way that in the acknowledgement of this presence we are also open to the outpourings of His love—not as if we were there to "draw from" His love, but the "fallout" is inevitable.

A setting for a filling station commercial was being readied in Hollywood. In order to be realistic it was set up along the street in the scene of passing traffic. Its station, pumps, and signs were indistinguishable from the genuine establishment. It was not too surprising that, while cameras were being positioned, people would pull up with their cars and ask for a tankful of gasoline. The actors, in their filling-station uniforms, turned many such cars away within the hour. Finally, one actor with a certain whimsy, decided to relieve the ennui by enacting the following charade.

Another car pulled up. The man rolled down his window and said, "Fill 'er up." The "attendant" politely complied by placing the nozzle of the hose into the tank and, while wiping the windows, pretended that he was dispensing gasoline out of the empty pump. When he was finished, he approached the car window, and the customer asked, "How much is it?" The "attendant" replied, "You are the one hundredth customer today, so we're giving it to you free of charge." The man drove off in his car grinning at his good fortune, apparently never bothering to check his gauge.

A parable for the Gathered Church leaps out of this. "He came empty and he went empty away." How many come among us in their condition of emptiness and depart even emptier because they find no evidence of the power and presence of God in the midst of His people? They have, unfortunately, encountered a dead congregation whose self-recognition as the Easter people has dwindled, and who have no excitement over the presence of their Lord.

In the renewal of the Church there is a strong emphasis upon the role of the laity. One denomination refers to lay people as the "ninety-nine percenters," because only about one percent of the Church consists of clergy. This renewal of lay participation has its expression in the acts of worship as well as in other aspects of Church life. The worship of the Church comes alive when the lay people know that they carry the largest responsibility for filling the fellowship with faith, fervor, and praise. They are the community who are risen with Christ and who are seeking those things which are above. They shall be called "the Easter people" from time to time as a reminder of the glorified state of life which they share in the resurrection of the Lord Jesus Christ.

There is another dimension to the Great Prayer, worship, which needs to be understood. It sounds mystical upon first hearing, but it is completely in accord with the common, yet uncommon, experience of fervent worshipers. That is to say, there are those present in the act of worship who must be described in more exalted terms than are used for the clergy and lay people who are gathered together.

Let the following story express this dimension. It is told by the Rev. Louis Tucker, an Episcopal clergyman, who tells of his life as a parish priest in a book called *Clerical Errors.* * I visited St. James Church in Baton Rouge, Louisiana, where this took place and I must say I had a feeling of *déjà vu*, having been there before, so strong was the impression of Tucker's experience upon me.

He was accustomed to having the service of Evensong every Sunday evening. It had, however, become a discouraging experience because only a few people came and these were, for the most part, elderly ladies. Not that they were not lovable or worthy, but he longed for greater participation by parishioners and the presence of men.

Before he entered he knelt and said a desperate prayer that he might somehow get through the service again, that there would be some sign of hope and meaning in it all. As he knelt at the prayer desk in the chancel, his eyes opened to an

---

*Louis Tucker, *Clerical Errors,* (New York and London: Harper and Brothers, 1943), pp. 207–209.

amazing sight. The church was full. The pews were all occupied. So great was the overflow that persons were standing about the nave. Then he became aware that they were angelic beings. They were young men with strong faces. He pinched himself to make sure he was not dreaming. At the altar there was also a presence upon which he did not feel worthy to fix his gaze. Not only were they there but they took part in the service, making strong responses. Somehow he knew that the few women who were present from the parish could not see or hear them.

His simple prayer had been answered in a remarkably profound way. He no longer would question the worthwhileness of the act of worship no matter how few in number were the people who gathered there. Any act of worship is worthwhile for the hosts of heaven are always there.

This has deeply affected my understanding of what takes place in the Great Prayer, the worship of the Gathered Church. It is my understanding that we are surrounded by far more than stained glass, wooden pews, and the people who occupy them. We are in the presence of angels and archangels and all the company of heaven.

Added to this is the precious meaning of the Communion of Saints, to which all who recite the Apostle's Creed give assent. It is the experience of many who engage in worship, and often in the Holy Communion, that those who have died in the faith are also in that company. They feel a definite closeness to those who have gone before. It has no relationship to spiritualism or the invocation of their presence through mediums. It is simply a dimension of the promise made to all the members of His body, that we all live in His household together, though some reside in other parts of the house where we are yet to visit.

It gives present meaning to the words of Hebrews 12:1–2: "Therefore, since we die surrounded by so great a cloud of witnesses, let us also lay aside every weight, and sin which clings so closely, and let us run with perseverance the race that is set before us, looking to Jesus the pioneer and perfecter of our faith, who for the joy that was set before him endured the cross, despising the shame, and is seated at the right hand of the throne of God."

2 Prayer
in the Apostolic Group

To be a member of the Body of Christ, the Church, is to be a person of prayer not only in the Gathered Church but also in the small group which I will call the Apostolic Group.

One of the great signs of the renewal of the Church in our time has been the new spiritual vitality found in the group movement, particularly in prayer groups. Investigations made of fast-growing congregations have revealed one common factor, that of vital small groups where people discover the working of the Holy Spirit in a kind of sharing of loving which is reminiscent of descriptions of the New Testament Church.

For many this has been a missing link in their prayer experience. On one hand, they may have discovered some of the wonder in the mystery of corporate worship. On the other hand, they may be fairly comfortable with occasional acts of individual prayer. That there is a logical link between the large body of people and being alone is missed by many in their churchmanship. This is the small group where there is neither the normal setting of the Sunday service nor the isolation of "prayer in the closet."

The prayer group is called the Apostolic Group because

it has its roots in the experiences of Jesus and His apostles. We recognize in His ministry the same dimensions of prayer that we observe in our own time—the large gatherings of people in the synagogues or on the hillsides, the lone experiences of prayer in the wilderness; and between them, the small group interrelationships with the Twelve. The latter was quite distinct from the other dimensions. Here there was a level of sharing and caring that was more pointed and intimate. Prayers evolved directly out of their experiences together or out of their preparations for them. They gathered at homes, by the Sea of Galilee, or as they paused on a journey. There was a teaching of the spiritual life that was closely wedded to their daily encounters with Pharisees, publicans, the sick, the disturbed, the sinful, and the seekers. At all times Jesus was the acknowledged leader of the small group. The apostles probably thought of it as an extension of the *hăborim,* the small groups that were related to the synagogue.

Today prayer groups are an extension of the Apostolic Group. The same elements are there—a wholesome intimacy characterized by caring and sharing, a growing spiritual life born out of daily experiences, and a sense of reaching out to others along the way. The most important element is also still there—the leadership of Jesus Christ. He is still at the center of a good prayer group.

Often the question of leadership comes up in relation to a small group that meets week after week. Should someone assume that role within the group? In the healthiest groups, that question is resolved by constantly affirming the leadership of Jesus Christ. A group may move from home to home where the host of the house begins the devotions, so that there is a sharing of this responsibility among all the members, but in each place the leadership of Christ takes over. They do not simply pray to Him; He is praying *with* them. "Where two or three are gathered together in my name, there am I in the midst of them."

I had the most remarkable example of what this means in a parish in Ohio. During my rectorship there, a large number of prayer groups came into being. Some met early in the morning, others at midmorning, some at noon, and some in the evening. There were groups for women, for men, for business people downtown, and mixed groups of men and women. Invariably these groups had ecumenical dimensions. There was never any question about leadership. The acknowledgment of Jesus Christ as the focal Person in each group seemed to be accepted by common consent without any particular discussion.

It became noticeable to me that as participation in these groups increased, my counseling load went down. The apparent reason for this was that the members of the Apostolic Group were dealing with the needs and concerns of one another as they had never done before. It was the New Testament Church in action. Clergy, who sometimes seem to feel threatened by these small groups, need to acknowledge that lay people are much better equipped to answer the needs of other lay people than they are, even though the clergy may claim academic credentials for counseling.

Wives and mothers are most sensitive to the common experiences of other wives and mothers. Workers in offices or factories are better equipped to understand the feelings of those whose daily lives are exposed to those atmospheres. Young people invariably gain the confidence of other youth, whereas the advice of adults is often resented. Prayer groups can become powerful centers for wholeness. The need for forgiveness and absolution is constant, and it can be exercised best of all in a fellowship of concerned people. A prominent psychologist told me that it was in the small group that congregations had the best resource for bringing wholeness to people in the midst of a broken society. He said he dreaded sending his patients back into the very environment that fostered the sad condition that brought them to his office in the first place. He would like to refer them to groups of loving people who would accept them as they were. Better yet, they would not need to come to him in the first place if they could find such "healing" groups.

Not that prayer groups have pretensions of being therapy groups or, as some have suspected, "spill-the-guts" groups, but that true wholeness, which comes from holy living on a daily basis, can be found there.

Small prayer groups need not be simply those that are usually recognized as established fellowships within the framework of a parish. If the experience accorded by the dimension of the small group, as distinct from gathered worship or solo prayer, is one that is needed for a rounding out of the spiritual life, it need not be frustrated where established groups are not to be found. Any small church organization can (indeed, this is its calling in the Lord) be a group in prayer—the gathering of church school teachers, the altar guild, the vestry, or church board. Why should not these church leaders pray for the Lord's concerns? On other levels we ought to be able to assume that a diocesan or synodical council, a gathering of jurisdictional leaders will be in prayer. In the Apostolic Group these prayers would not only be for "church business" but for one another.

But the formation of small groups has even more obvious dimensions. Of these the family is the most obvious. More and more families are finding that it is possible to pray together. As natural as this seems to families who have always done it, it must be said that it is an undiscovered joy in many Christian families. Some confess embarrassment over the initiation of family prayers. With what seemed to constitute an act of courage at the outset, many more families are now finding that they can pray together (often spontaneously) around the breakfast table, at dinner, or before bedtime. There is probably no more simple explanation for the phenomenon of church-oriented children growing up to be totally secular adults than that there was no prayer in their household. They therefore automatically came to assume that religion had nothing to do with everyday life.

Another possibility remains for those who still haven't been able to break this barrier in the family. This is the prayer partner. One other person with yourself constitutes a prayer group. It is quite essential to spiritual growth that we have another human being who knows us well, who loves us as we are, and who can join with us in prayer at almost any time. It is important that there be someone with whom we can share our spiritual concerns and whose prayers will bolster ours. It is too easy to hide from the recognition of our growing edge in the relative anonymity of the pew or the solitariness of our closet.

One particular men's prayer group met every Tuesday morning at 6:30. Such was their devotion, built upon the effects of prayer, upon their workaday lives, that neither bad weather nor holiday would deter them from getting together each week in one another's homes. They had nothing in common except their prayer fellowship, for they were of varying personalities and vocations. Among them were: a plumber, an artist, doctors, lawyers, teachers, an engineer, executives, and workers.

Their effectiveness as an Apostolic Group was demonstrated, not only in the way they reached out to people in their spheres of influence but by the way they articulated their faith in various panel groups in churches throughout the state. They had no training in speaking, but when they simply told of the many ways in which they knew the presence of Jesus Christ in day-by-day work and in family life, they recruited untold numbers into a practicing prayer life. The very nonprofessional nature of their presentations gave strength to the appeal for a life in communion with God. They had no ax to grind, only a story to tell.

About a year after I left that parish to go to Kansas City, I communicated with these men and those of another active prayer group. I asked if they would come to assist me with a men's retreat at a place near Kansas City. Their slogan, "Have faith, will travel," still held true. Several carloads of these men came at their own expense, traveling more than a thousand miles.

At that time there was a small beginning of prayer group activity at that church in Kansas City. One group had recently begun after I had prayed for such a fellowship for six months. A young stock broker, who had had a dramatic conversion experience on the streets of that city, finally approached me to ask if a prayer group could be started. He offered to bring one other man to my home the following morning. Although he himself did not arrive, having overslept, the other man did—but it was a beginning. The next week he was there with several other men. It was this nucleus that came to the retreat with the Apostolic Group from Ohio.

The great spiritual principle of faith-contagion held true at that retreat. The strong testimony of their willingness to make this great effort to be there, for no other reason than their vital experience of God's love through prayer, would have been sufficient. Added to that were the stories of those everyday encounters with the Spirit of God, which had a galvanizing effect upon their hearers. Such a fire was set that within another year more than seventy men were involved in a number of prayer groups in that Kansas City church.

Again, the spirit of this lay apostleship in prayer was demonstrated when I moved to Minnesota. The passage of time had not diminished their moving love of God. Having gathered together a small assembly of men from the northern parish, I proceeded to invite men from both Ohio and Missouri to join in a retreat at that fairly distant location. From both places, by car and plane, they came with an eagerness to share their prayer life with others. Great expense in time and money were involved in round trips of a thousand miles.

The effect was the same as before. Lives were permanently affected and new apostolic groups were formed by the stories of living faith told by people who carried their most precious credential, their renewed life under the management of Jesus Christ.

Out of the Ohio groups, stories of life-changing experiences would in themselves fill a book. One example is the story of a man we will call Larry. He had come to a point of despondency in his life, having reached a bewildering crisis involving his personal life, and terrifying feelings of self-accusation. His work was totally without meaning to him. What frail faith in God he ever had was gone. He went out in his car at night to end his life. As he approached a bridge abutment, he floored the accelerator and aimed the car at the solid point of instant obliteration. In the split second before he would have crashed he prayed a last-second desperation prayer, "God, if you are real and if you love me, come to me now." In that moment he was flooded with the peace of God and averted his self-destruction.

He became a strong part of the Apostolic Group after that. He had come to Kansas City with the others, and on a gravel road at the retreat place he told me that he had been called to the ministry. I didn't need to remind him that, with a family of four to support, he would have two more years of college to complete and then three years of seminary. He knew this. Today he is active in the ordained ministry.

Lest it be thought that the Apostolic Group is just for men, this additional story: Sister Grace, as we shall call her, came to this Ohio parish to speak to the women of the parish about life in a convent. Her story was particularly interesting because she had been a rising young star in Hollywood, and she was particularly recognizable through a popular television series. With this career going strong she felt a call to an Episcopal order while still in her twenties. Now, dressed in her habit, she came to this parish to tell of the religious life.

Having arrived the previous evening, she had a free morning before her afternoon address. Learning that my wife, Marj, was to be in a small prayer group in the forenoon, she asked if she might attend. "Of course," Marj said, "but I'm afraid it won't be much of an experience for you, considering your background." The group met at one of the homes and followed its spontaneous format of prayers, sharing, and study. It was obvious to any onlooker that they had no theological pretensions nor did they display any unnatural piosity. There was no doubt that they loved one another as they were, though they were not content with remaining at that level of growth. If one knew the stories of those present, they would tell of reaching out to many who had been unchurched, without faith, in a crisis of life. In short, they were an Apostolic Group.

When lunchtime came, and my wife brought Sister Grace to the meeting at the church, I asked how things had gone at the prayer group. She said, "I think it must have been boring for Sister Grace because she didn't say a word." After lunch, Sister Grace went to the podium to deliver her address. Pointedly laying aside her notes, she said, "I have had the most remarkable experience of prayer this morning that I have ever had in my whole life; therefore I'm discarding everything I had planned to say to you today in order to speak of what happened there." Then she went on to tell at some length of how moved she was by the love expressed in that small group, the down-to-earth faith, and the sense of expectation of the Lord's goodness. She said, "I felt the presence of the hosts of heaven in that small group."

It was not to be a fly-by-night emotional response, for as she returned to her work with teenagers from troubled homes, she found that this way of prayer was a breakthrough in many broken hearts and relationships. In small groups or face-to-face opportunities for spontaneous prayer, she found out for the first time what was "eating" many of these young people. Together with this came a new channel of communication with the God of help.

3 Prayer in the Scattered Church

Perhaps by this time we have overcome that naïvete which once looked upon the Church as simply that building on the corner where certain spiritual and social activities took place. We will, we hope, find it a cliché in our day to remind people that the Church is the Body of Christ, and that the Church exists wherever the members of that Body go. This is what is meant by the Scattered Church. It is the recognition that the Church is represented in the world at large by those who live in Christ. It is the antidote to that kind of parochialism that can't think of "Church" except in terms of parish functions.

The Scattered Church is also the story of our individual, separated existence, which we must live out on the daily scene of employment, family, recreation, community, and our own aloneness. It is life in the secular world, but it is lived with a sense of divine mission.

This chapter emphasizes the individual prayer life of the member of Christ. Some may understand this as "personal prayer," but this is an inadequate concept if it merely covers the devotional practices of the private person. In thinking of the prayer life of the Scattered Church, we are dealing with a life "in Christ" on a constant basis.

When St. Paul's experience of individual churchmanship was described in terms of "being in Christ," it encompassed an expression of prayer which was more than intermittent. Paul was often required to "go it alone." For a time Mark was his companion, and then Luke was with him for a longer time. He also had occasions of deep fellowship with embryonic congregations in Asia Minor and Macedonia. However, much of his time was spent alone. The words of 2 Corinthians 11:25–28 speak of this: "Three times I have been shipwrecked; a night and a day I have been adrift at sea; on frequent journeys, in danger from rivers, danger from robbers, danger from my own people, danger from Gentiles, danger in the city, danger in the wilderness, danger at sea, danger from false brethren; in toil and hardship, through many a sleepless night, in hunger and thirst, often without food, in cold and exposure." He is speaking not only of hardship but aloneness. But in all of this he could speak of "being in Christ." This truth is profoundly important for today's Christian, who lives most of his hours without the visible support of fellowship. It means that prayer life must be effective on the individual level. Daily life is the testing ground of our relationship with Jesus Christ. There is no substitute for firsthand communication with Him. We need to stop humoring those husbands who say with sardonic seriousness, "I don't need religion, my wife has enough for both of us." Secondhand faith doesn't work. This is the meaning of the expression: "God has no grandchildren; only children."

Another of the great signs of renewal in our time is the affirmation of the importance of a personal relationship with Jesus Christ. For some this is, surprisingly, a new discovery. They had thought of their churchmanship as having something to do with certain church programs, but the thought of a personal relationship with Christ smacked of a kind of religiosity which they associated with fanatics or backwoods pietists. Now, people of sophistication have come to a strong sense of the meaning of this kind of devotion. On the other hand, those for whom the jargon of personal piety was often saccharine, sentimental, and otherwordly have come to see this relationship as one which penetrates their style of life on every conceivable level.

If we consider the way in which Jesus encountered His followers, it is not surprising that this personal relationship is of a high order of importance. When Jesus wished to select His followers, He did not beckon to some vague shadowy group looming on the horizon and say, "Hey group, come and follow me." Rather, He came face to face individually with Andrew and Peter and James and John and the others, establishing a relationship that was personalized to the core of their being. They would know Him as a group, but they would always know and be known under their individual identities. This, then, has everything to do with our prayer life in the Scattered Church.

If we understand that "being in Christ" is descriptive of a life lived in this total surrounding presence, analogous to a fish living in water—buoyed up by it, moving within it, straining it through its gills for absolute substenance of life—then we should not be surprised that in some real measure our lives become a recapitulation of His. The pattern of our life in Him will give us that strong sense of companionship that His disciples felt. We will also be led to the wilderness of temptation. Then, again, we shall find ourselves on the Mount of Transfiguration—a mountaintop experience which can never be erased. He did not promise that our life with Him would be without tribulation, so He also leads us to the Garden of Gethsemane. There we may find that we have to relinquish more than we had ever dreamed necessary in order that His will may be done and not ours. This could lead us to our own Calvary when we need to die to that within ourselves which made surrender so painful at Gethsemane. But always—always—there is the resurrection. He bids us to rise up, forgiven, restored, renewed.

This recapitulation of Christ's life in the Scattered Church need not be thought of in terms of a long extension of time, such as being spread out over a total lifetime. All of this could happen within an hour. We may rise up with optimism, the world in happy submission, only to be dashed to the ground a few minutes later by a few words in a letter. This may quickly lead us to a reexamination of our souls to see what it is that needs to be crucified within us, what it is that would cause such a devastating reaction to a momentary crisis. But again, the resurrection—always the resurrection —for we are the Easter people! He leads us to a style of living that would not allow us to grovel in despair or defeat, but in which He says, "Arise, my child, get on with my work."

What this inevitably comes to mean is living with expectation. The wordly man has no reason to look at life except in terms of growing, ever-verified, cynicism. But he whose life is one of communication with a Lord who is always accessible learns to live on a level of hopeful expectation. Expectations increase as trust grows. Trust grows as answers become more frequent. Someone has said, "To live as a Christian without expectation is blasphemous." In truth, it would be to deny the very nature of the God of love. Love is not abstract: it is concretely expressed in the lives of those who are open to His good will.

Critics will be quick to observe that this life of expectation is easy for those who are healthy, prosperous, and popular. But what of those less fortunate? When I was leading a prayer conference in Minnesota, I was asked by a clergyman to make a call upon a lady who had been ill for a long time. I went to her home and discovered a middle-aged woman— we'll call her Maggie—who had suffered from a spinal defect all her life. She was not more than four feet tall and quite deformed. And yet, as soon as you saw her you were met by a radiant smile, an inwardly victorious beauty. Who, in this world of physically conscious romanticism, would have expected such a woman to marry? And yet she had. Her husband was a handsome and compassionate man. Less likely, by medical prognostication, would be that that tiny body, no more than seventy pounds, would bear a child. But she had, a normal and lovely girl. Why all this, with so little in the original grant of earthly life? It was because she lived a life of faithful expectation.

Beyond this, she had become a servant of the Lord by teaching Church School children on the nursery level. So effective was Maggie with these little people that years later they would come to her home to see her. How many nursery teachers can claim this kind of lasting affection? She even capitalized on the physical fact of being so close to their size.

At this visit she gave me a copy of some thoughts that had come to her as she had been deeply in prayer during this most recent illness:

Be not afraid my child, for I am with you always. Know that I will take care of your every need, comfort you when in pain. I gave you life so that, in giving it back to me, you will know you will live forever and praise my name. Yes, and know that suffering will come to you because you have chosen to love me through my son Jesus Christ. Continue to reach out to me so that you may feel my healing power, and let my gentle commands be heavenly music to your ears. Remember that I allowed you to give life when earthly man told you this was not possible, but I wanted man to know that miracles can happen to anyone who has faith in me, and knows I am almighty and powerful. Have you forgotten there are those with perfect vision who are yet blind to my promises? I will use my almighty power to reach all my flock. Know that I have performed many miracles in your life, so that you would be a living witness for me. There are those that need to see visual signs of my miracles to believe. They see in you the love, the compassion, the strength a child of God can experience through suffering. You, my child, have been chosen because I love you, and you have returned my love. Fear not. Praise my name to all people, and know I am with you always.

The obvious truth which surrounds the life of each of us in the Scattered Church is that we come into this world single file and we leave single file. It is to live in such communion with Him along the way from our entry to our exit that we can truly be an Easter person in all spheres of daily contact, knowing that God and one person are a majority anywhere.

There is also the importance of being able to live each day as if it were our last. This is a morbid thought except for those who are conscious of having a constant grip upon the timeless life of Christ. To live each day as if it were our last (for well it might be, and one is sure to be) is not to live detached from wordly considerations, but to be much better equipped to deal with them on the basis of reality—the reality of our temporariness here. It also exalts each day with the knowledge that we are always on the brink of the Great Adventure. It teaches us to value each hour, and not to leave our house cat-kicking and door-slamming. Life is too precious to be wasted on our trivial resentments and moods.

4 Being and Praying

If you are to be a person who lives in communication with the Triune God, whether in the Gathered Church, the Apostolic Group, or the Scattered Church, you must come to terms with your own being. Your self-image has everything to do with your life of prayer.

Everyone has to live inside himself. Did you ever feel that your eyes were simply windows, and that you were looking out at the world as a spectator inside a moving or standing booth? That day, everywhere you might go, you would have a strange feeling about being yourself. You might reflect to yourself, "Can this really be myself who is standing here? Can this really be myself whose voice is coming out of this mouth? Does that other person feel as I do, or is his world totally different?"

Your self-image is bound up with your prayer life. There are different attitudes you can have about selfhood. For instance, to be sick of yourself. There are various kinds of sickness, but one of the worst is to be sick of yourself. You hate what you see in the mirror in the morning, the sound of your own voice, the way you walk, the way you think you appear to others. You feel that you are boring; you even bore yourself. You drag through your days wishing you were someone else. But you can't be, and so you continue to be a prisoner of your dull self.

No one compliments you to make you feel any better about yourself. You meet an acquaintance on the street who says, "My, you look like death warmed over. Is something wrong with you?" You wish someone would point out that there is something right with you.

Perhaps you have lived more than half your life and you have the sobering realization that you have left no real mark on the world. You thought you had some special talent when you were young, that your life would become like a recognized work of art. Now you discover that it has only been graffiti scribbled on the wall of time. No wonder you are sick of yourself. You cannot have any kind of prayer life in this state of being.

This is seeing yourself as you really are. Self-acceptance can only come by faith in the saving grace of Jesus Christ. You can see yourself just as He sees you. You may not have movie star looks. It makes no difference to Him, or to people who are on His wave length. You may not seem to be too intelligent, but Christ is infinitely brilliant and passes on His wisdom to you. Others may have different expectations of you, but you are yourself and not what they wish you would be.

You fall short of the glory of God—you know it, and the Lord knows it. But He doesn't throw up His hands; He extends His hands. The young may think you are worthless because you are old. The old may think you are worthless because you are young. But your age makes no difference to Christ, and therefore it comes to make no difference to you. You have self-acceptance because He accepts you.

People may despise you, but they despised Him first, and you can whistle gaily in the knowledge that you are a child of the King. He will speak to you, and you may speak to

Him. You can learn patience with your rate of spiritual growth. You don't have to dig up the roots every day to see if they are still growing. You only torture and kill them that way.

You can also accept others as they are, not as you wish they would be. If Christ loves you the way you are, He must love them in the same way. You don't have to be sick of yourself. You are precious to Him. I have seen plain faces light up into new beauty upon this realization.

A young lady I will call Fran came to my office one day. She lived in the fast-moving society of the professional football crowd. Her husband was a big-name football player, so their social whirl was identified with this rather glamorous "in group." Most football wives, it seemed, were former cheer leaders with sparkling personalities and good looks. Fran didn't quite fit into this category. In fact she was quite plain, and she struggled to enjoy the late-night parties and swinging times the others seemed to find so entertaining. She complained to me that this social whirl seemed so artificial. When the parties were over and all the noise ceased, she had a terribly empty feeling. She wondered if she were a misfit in the world, a disappointment to her husband, and a drag on her friends.

It soon became apparent that this was a spiritual matter. What did she really want out of life? What did acceptance mean on a deeper level—the approval of a certain crowd, or a recognition of her own selfhood? I told her that she was infinitely precious in the eyes of Jesus Christ. He loved her as she was and would take her to new levels of promise. This truth came to her with an amazing suddenness. For her it was a conversion. With tear-filled eyes she accepted Christ's acceptance. We both knew that He was in that room with us pouring out His love.

The next day she was with one of her friends having a cup of coffee. The friend declared, "You look so beautiful today.

What beauty parlor are you going to?" Fran simply spoke of her experience of the previous day. She met a level of spiritual understanding with her football-wife friend that they had never achieved at the cocktail parties. She too, it turned out, was utterly bored with that forced gaiety. In the weeks and months to come, others noticed this new radiance in Fran and began asking about it. It was the beginning of a neighborhood spiritual movement. Fran also took an important role in the life of the parish and, within a year, her husband and children were deeply involved.

With self-acceptance in Christ you can become a person of prayer. You find that you don't have to be sick of yourself. And you don't have to be an egotist, taking yourself overseriously in the futile exercise of self-adoration. You don't have to impress people. You don't have to be a success. Jesus Christ was the biggest failure in the world, as viewed by common human standards. He was despised and rejected by people, but He knew where He had come from. His mission was to save these very people, both the browbeaten and the proud.

Knowing this, we can be the kind of people who can communicate with Him in prayer—neither too unworthy-feeling nor too vain. But self-acceptance, though it opens the way to prayer, is not the final step in the process. We move, through union with Christ, from self-acceptance to self-offering. We do not know we have a self worth offering until we discover we have a self worth accepting. We discover that we can afford to give away our life in surrender to Christ and in self-offering for others. We do not have to protect our little place in the world like a cornered rat fighting his last-ditch battle. "He who loses his life for my sake and the Gospel will find it," Jesus said. And He meant it. It really works.

A teen-ager, along with her father, was at an evening prayer-group session at our home, and she brought this point home when she made a personal reflection upon the meaning of the Christian life of self-offering. We were engaged in a discussion of greed and possessiveness. She said, "If another girl asked to use my sweater and, in love, I let her use it, it becomes much more valuable than if I tried to keep it. What I give away is worth much more than the love I keep." How deeply her father and the rest of us were moved to see this Christian insight in one so young! A few weeks later, at a prayer retreat, I had the privilege of baptizing this family in the icy waters of Lake Superior.

The truly content and serene people of this world are those who are set free to live lives of self-offering. The more of themselves they give, the more of themselves they have. And thus it was that Christ was so immensely radiant. People were drawn to His side because they instinctively knew He had something infinitely valuable that He was willing to give away—it was His very life.

To recapitulate: You don't give yourself away if you are sick of yourself and feel worthless, and you can't pray while in this state. You won't be motivated to give yourself away if you feel egotistic and expect the world to wait upon you, and you won't pray if you don't believe you need improvement. But if you find out that you are precious to God even as you are, and if He can accept you, you certainly have no business not accepting yourself. You can find yourself in the fullest communion with Him. And then, indeed, you have a life worth offering up to Him and to others who are equally precious to Him.

Cuthbert Bardsley, Bishop of Coventry, tells of a man who was continually in an alternating state of drunkenness and repentance. The bishop had him on his prayer list for about ten years, but the cycle seemed unbroken. With his prayer list growing, the bishop finally asked God, "May I take that man off my list?" But God clearly indicated to him that he should keep him in his prayers. The selfhood of this weak man was still precious to the Lord. In that tenth year the man finally made a commitment of his life to God that was to be lasting. He was to become one of the most effective members of the Church and particularly dedicated to intercessory prayer. It was a reminder that we must continually offer ourselves and our prayers for those who as yet do not know of their worth to Christ. When they find this out they also can become self-offerings for others. When we know Christ's love for us, we also have more compassion on others, even the unlovely.

The episode between Jesus and Peter following the Resurrection illustrates this whole chapter. This is found in John 21:15: "When they had finished breakfast, Jesus said to Simon Peter, 'Simon, son of John, do you love me more than these?' He said to Him, 'Yes, Lord, you know that I love you.'" Two more times Jesus asked Peter if he loved Him. And Peter, who fully and grievously remembered that he had denied Jesus three times, and now was being given three opportunities to express his love, said, "Lord, you know everything; you know that I love you." Peter had once been proud and self-protective. He was always the one with the answers. Close to the time of the passion he had declared, "Even if you go to death, I will not leave you." Here was Peter the egotist.

But it was not long until he would deny Christ three times. All his bravery was gone. No sooner had he made this denial than he became sick of himself. He went and cried bitterly when he realized the sad truth of what he had done and what it revealed of his shabby character.

Now, in this post-Resurrection encounter with the Lord, came the third phase of Peter's selfhood and a new level of communication. He found himself loved and accepted by Christ even as he was. He no longer had to go about with that inner sickness of disgust, because he was forgiven and restored. This new, realistic kind of communication made it possible for him to move on to the fourth stage; that of becoming a self-offering to feed Christ's sheep. It was predicted by the Lord in that same encounter: " 'When you are old, you will stretch out your hands and another will gird you and carry you where you do not wish to go.' (This he said to show by what death he was to glorify God.) And after this he said to him, 'Follow me' " (Jn. 21:18–19). A new self had been born, one in whom Christ lived.

5 Dealing with Our Voices

When you discover the value of your being in God's eyes, you begin to discover the value of your inner voices. Do you hear voices speaking within you? You may say, "I hope not; only insane people hear voices." But think again: Is there not a voice speaking within you at this very moment? Perhaps it is saying something like this: "What is he getting at? What does he mean, 'Do I hear voices?' "

The fact is that there are voices speaking within us all day long. We have often referred to this as "thinking," but that is just an arbitrary reference to a phenomenon which is much more profound than simple cerebration. It behooves us to become more conscious of the fact that there are voices speaking within us every waking and sleeping moment if we are to be more fully aware of our place in the Praying Church. There are voices with definite expression and emphasis, voices that sometimes give long discourses, and that utter sharp ejaculatory remarks at other times.

Whose voices are they? Your own, of course. When people begin hearing voices of other people—unseen people—they may be suspicious of having some serious emotional illness. But in spite of the observation that the voice you hear is your own, there is still more than one voice within you. There are at least three, three that are speaking at different levels, three that are speaking from different parts of you.

For instance, one voice will be saying as you are on your way to work on a Monday morning, "I could not seriously think of not going to work; it's necessary in order to earn a living." Immediately, another voice will say, "I would really rather stay at home and sleep all day." After that a third voice will ask pulsing questions: "What is it all about anyway? What am I working for? What does it all mean?" An echo of that voice also says, "I'm really a little scared."

Take another example. You are about to launch out on a recreational activity which you used to think was a great deal of fun. The first voice says: "I'm going to go ahead and do this. I can still get some fun out of it. Besides, recreation is good for me." The second voice says: "Let's face it, I don't really get the kick out of it that I used to. I wonder if I should even make the effort." The third voice then chimes in with something quite jolting and strange: "I'm lonesome. I'm really very lonesome in a profound way, and none of this really fulfills my deepest needs."

What are these three contending voices? The first is the voice of your mind. It speaks to you of what is rational and expedient, of what is necessary, or at least reasonably expected of you. "I ought to work, therefore I will." The second is the voice of your body. "I feel more like sleeping." It speaks to you of your feelings, drives and energies. The third is the voice of your spirit. "Why work, anyhow? What's it about?" It speaks of your meaning, your destiny, your hopes, your fears, your infinite longings. Don't assume that just because there is a spiritual part of you speaking within yourself that this is necessarily a holy spirit. The spiritual part of us can be as sick or as whole as our mind or body.

This is where a fourth voice comes in, a fourth voice that will save us from the disintegrating disagreement among our three voices, a fourth voice that will speak to our spirit which bears the responsibility of telling our body what its real purpose is, what it was made for, and of telling our mind what thoughts are constructive and what thoughts are destructive. That fourth voice is not our own, although it becomes everything to us. That voice is consistent and steady, good and holy. It is the voice of God as He reveals Himself to us in Jesus Christ. It is prayer. His Holy Spirit speaks to our spirit.

When Peter, James, and John had seen Jesus on the Mount of the Transfiguration, the voice from heaven said, "This is my beloved Son, listen to Him." This they did, but not until He was crucified, risen, and had poured out the Holy Spirit upon them. Before that they were having great trouble with their own voices. The truth of what Jesus said about the Pharisee now makes sense to us, "And the Pharisee prayed thus *to himself.*" He heard his own self-congratulatory voice, but he was not in communication with God.

After Pentecost they listened to Him every step of the way. They became a Praying Church, and because they lived by this kind of communication the Body of Christ became a reality wherever they went.

Delving more deeply into this, we ask: "How does the voice of the Son speak to our spirit?" Through the God-given process of prayer. This process of submissive listening also takes place as we prayerfully read the Holy Scriptures. He also speaks to our spirit in the act of worship. We need cōnstantly to remind ourselves that worship is prayer. As we become more sensitized to His love for humanity by our more constant association with the Incarnate One, He also speaks to us through the needs of others.

He speaks to us in stillness before Him. Elijah, having come to the mountain with his complaint that he alone was left to seek the Lord's will, had come to the point in his life where he was listening only to his own voices. The way of communication had staled by his fierce activism. In the reverie of his own misery he was jarred by the sudden tremors of an earthquake. His bombastic life led him to believe that the Lord was now speaking to him through this cataclysmic event. But He wasn't. There was also a tremendous cyclone which scattered the rocks and dust around his face. Surely, the God of force was speaking in the howling wind. But He wasn't. Then a searing fire raced over the face of the mountain. Would not God be speaking to him in that blazing heat? But he wasn't. Then all the sounds and furies ceased, and God spoke to him in a still small voice. Listening in the stillness is an essential part of our prayer experience. One great Christian once said, "God has given us one mouth but two ears; therefore, in our prayers we ought to listen twice as long as we speak."

As we listen, what does He say to our minds? "Have this mind in you which is in Christ Jesus" (Phil. 2:5). "Do not be conformed to this world, but be transformed by the renewal of your mind, that you may prove what is the will of God, what is good and acceptable and perfect" (Rom. 12:2). "In everything by prayer and supplication with thanksgiving let your requests be made known to God. And the peace of God, which passes all understanding, will keep your hearts and your minds in Christ Jesus" (Phil. 4:6–7).

He does not restrict or shrivel the use of the mind. He expands it and sets it free, for God's thoughts are always greater than our own thoughts could ever be. Our thoughts are no longer circular within ourselves, but they go out to the Eternal God and back to us again.

As we listen to the Beloved Son, what does He say to our bodies? "Present your bodies as a living sacrifice . . . which is your spiritual worship" (Rom. 12:1). A sacrificial offering is that which is laid upon the altar of God to be made holy. "Your body is the temple of the Holy Spirit." (1 Cor. 3:16). A temple is where prayer takes place. In other words, in no way can we take this popular stance, "It's my own body; I can do what I want with it. I'm only hurting myself, so what's the difference?"

People get very confused about the body. They may think it is merely a bundle of appetites that must be satisfied. They may think it is an object of adoration that must be given comfort and pampering. Yes, these are the things which the voice of the body wants to say to us. But then, listen to the voice of the Lord, who says, in effect: "Your body is given to serve me and to serve my other children. The eyes of a Christian have a different outlook than those of the self-server. The mouth of a Christian speaks in distinctly different tones than the self-server. The ears hear different things, the biddings of God. The hands hold and convey different things: mercy to others, offerings to my altar. The feet convey you to different places: to places of need, to the House of God." The fact of the Incarnation tells us for all time that the human lives around us are precious in His sight.

Then, as we listen to the Beloved Son, what does He say to our spirits? He says, "God is spirit, and those who worship him must worship in spirit and in truth" (Jn. 4:24). To worship means to acknowledge God as the All in All, the one without whom our spirit cannot be at rest. The deepest warfare within us, and the loudest, most disturbing voice, will not be quieted until the spirit finds its true home in Him, its home in the one who gave that spirit, and the one who will keep that spirit even when this physical body is no more.

A devoted member of one of the Kansas City prayer groups had not always known the truth either about his own inner voices or, particularly, the voice of God. His life was indeed filled with voices, for he was employed in the communication tower of a great airport. All day long he heard one voice after the other as planes prepared for landing or take-off. His addiction to voices extended to his travel in his car to and from the airport as he played his radio full blast. After he had learned the value of prayer he sought the voice of the Lord, particularly in the creative use of silence. He said, "Now I tune out my radio, my own disruptive thoughts, and tune in God."

What do you do about your voices, for undoubtedly we all have them? Do you listen to them with a mixture of hope and despair? Assuredly, there is no suggestion here that we should not hear what we are saying to ourselves so that we may measure where we are and where we ought to be. Or do you try to drown out your voices with nervous activity, noise, and numbing chemicals? Or can you, with healthy repentance, tune out your locked-in self and then listen to the voice of Christ? "This is my beloved Son, listen to Him." The Praying Church lets Him speak to mind, body, and spirit.

> Lord, speak to me, that I may speak
> In living echoes of thy tone;
> As thou has sought, so let me seek
> Thy erring children lost and lone.
>
> O fill me with thy fulness, Lord,
> Until my very heart oerflow
> In kindling thought and glowing word
> Thy love to tell, thy praise to show.

6 Prayer in a Scientific Age

Where does the Praying Church find itself in relation to the scientific age in the last quarter of the twentieth century? This was the century when some scientists predicted that the increase of science would bring about the decrease in religion. The practice of prayer would be one of the first things to go as dependence upon the supernatural was discredited by the ever-increasing numbers of educated people who would solve their problems by inductive and deductive reasoning. One of the favorite ways for sociologists to speak of religion was that "man needs religion in order to explain the unknown." Then, as the theory went, science would successfully continue to push back the borders of the unknown. Finally, when all that is now unexplainable became fully explained, there would no longer be any need for religion.

Now we are beginning to hear a new theme, and it comes from scientists themselves. Many of the greatest people of science have discovered that religion is not needed for the unknown as much as it is needed for that which is known. Faith is needed to live the life that is required by a scientific and technological world. Beyond that, the truly important questions cannot be resolved by science—questions of mean-

ing, love relationships, and death. New respect for the matters of prayer arises from these academic circles when they
see that faith is not a "pie in the sky by and by" matter, but
that which deals with moment-by-moment living in this
world.

Not long ago I met a noted scientist when I was giving a
retreat at a great university center. The other members of the
scientific community who were present were surprised to see
her there because she had not been seen in religious circles.
Everyone was quite awed by her world-renowned status and
the fact that she had earned four doctorates in scientific
fields. She was there because she had found that all her
extensive resources of scientific knowledge could not deal
with the experiences she was now going through. Her husband had died a few months before. She had expected to
handle this by rational means, but she now realized that it
was impossible. Faced with the awesomeness of death, she
found herself barren of resources. For the first time, she was
questioning whether there was any meaning in what she had
been doing. Was there any ultimate sense to ordering and
arranging the natural order if there was no framework of
meaning out of the supernatural order?

She spent as much time as she could in private conversation with me, questioning me on all these matters. She got
to the point of admitting that she could not make the leap
from scientific reasoning to faith. Unless things could be
laboratory tested she could not believe them. How was she
to make the leap she knew she had to make to make sense
out of life? I began to tell her of the many great scientific
figures of our time who found they could become people of
faith and prayer without sacrificing their scientific careers.
There is Werner Von Braun, the space scientist, who had
searched as far as any man into the vast recesses of the
astronomical universe. His search brought about a strong
conviction that no mere accident could explain the majestic

beauty and harmony of the stars and planets. It became evident to him that a personal, benevolent Being stood behind and within creation. Faith had come, and the use of the mind was not lessened but quickened.

Then there is William Pollard, the atomic physicist who discovered that physical science, which he had once confidently assumed would answer all the world's needs in this century, was finite after all, It could go so far but no farther, and the most serious needs of mankind would never be met by this means. Physical science was already a mature science. It wasn't as if it were a field that was just opening up and that what might yet be discovered would overwhelm all thoughts of any other methods. Rather, the elemental chart was filled out and the real issues of life remained unresolved. He moved from agnosticism to Christian faith. Eventually he became an ordained priest of the Episcopal Church. He continued, however, to bear high credentials in the atomic research community. He was not denying his intellect by the leap of faith but expanding it.

The experience of Edward McCrady, cosmic biologist, was brought up. He had written some of the most significant scientific papers on the origins of the universe. When his most profound research was done and put into writing, he chanced to pick up a Bible one day and peruse the first chapters of Genesis. He was astounded. There was his thesis. Though Genesis had never been intended as a textbook on science but as a book of beginnings, more concerned with the "Who" than the "how," the aeons described in the process of creation were remarkably similar to the best scientific theories. Dr. McCrady, then becoming a committed Christian layman and president of the University of the South at Sewanee, delved more deeply into these amazing discoveries. As a scientist he knew that a basic tenet upon which scientific thought rested was that there could not be any observable effect in this world that did not also have an adequate cause.

While this sufficed to explain much of the physical phenomena of the world through various forces of action and reaction, there still needed to be more explanation of the most profound effect observable to man. What is the most significant phenomenon in this world? Is it gravitation? Is it procreation? Is it metamorphosis? No, the greatest observable matter in the world is far above force or biology; it is human personality. Its very existence must be explained in terms of an adequate cause. Not power, force, nor energy hold the key to this, because they are actually subservient to personality. The human imagination is even able to manipulate and change them. There must be a cause of personality which is in itself at least personal, or else there could be no such phenomenon in existence. Therefore, a personal God must be postulated for a rational explanation of life. It will not suffice, as some of the priestlings of the scientific world had offered, to refer to God as a mere source of power. Then He would not be as great as that which He has made. Dr. McCrady saw no reasonable choice except to believe in God. Inasmuch as the perfection of love, the greatest manifestation of personality, is seen in Jesus Christ, he knew that he must go the Christian way. If God is personal, then He is also approachable in prayer.

My scientist inquirer was intrigued, and she agreed to go further into these matters. Her eagerness was so intense that when the retreat was over she sought me out at a home where I was staying overnight and spent part of the evening asking searching questions about the meaning of the Crucifixion. This discussion touched her so much that she said, "I never understood this Christian teaching in this way. I would like to tape-record these thoughts and send them to a scientific friend in London." She asked me to come to her home on the following day to go into this further. I arrived at her lovely home far back in the woods, and as soon as I was in her living room she began asking me questions about the Bible. To tell of the whole Bible one hour before taking off in a plane! Impossible. But her brilliant mind was now moving swiftly upon the agenda of revelation. She was beginning to see that there need be no divorce between reason and revelation.

Prayer is no longer a matter of superstition or magic to the great minds of our time. Once science and religion had been at loggerheads. Now religion, on the one hand, is able to concede that science is simply describing in increasingly accurate terms the wonderful and orderly ways by which God works in His universe. Men of faith can see that God is not threatened or affronted by mental activity. He knows the measure of man's mind for He implanted its capabilities. He is not surprised. He is not pushed off His throne by man's discoveries. Those potentialities simply further display the incredibility of God's gifts to us.

On the other hand, science is able to concede that faith has validity. No reputable scientist looks at natural law as an immutable statute which defies change or variation. He only claims to be describing what at this time is observable about nature's regular activities. Nor can they look upon these so-called laws as forces that defy external interference. Actually these orderly ways of nature can be controlled and used by man. Prayer is admissible as one means of variation, just as much as other acts of humanity such as turning on a light switch.

When I was a child I loved to play outdoors during the spring thaws. At that season rivulets of water would run in new and surprising places, relentlessly seeking that lower level, finding creeks that would eventually feed into the Mississippi River, which would, according to nature's decree, flow into the Gulf of Mexico. With a little spade I would pack mud and slush in walls that would completely divert a stream so that it would turn in a new direction. It occurs to me that if a child with his little spade can divert these tremendous forces, how much more can God manipulate the forces of His own creation in answer to our prayers.

When we pray we are not asking God to violate the ordered logic of His universe, but we are asking Him to respond in accordance with His will, so that He will make use of the ways He has established with the many variations which He alone could design. After all, they are His own laws, and He did not make them in such a way that they would frustrate His loving response to us. His laws are not of a higher order than His love. When, occasionally, in response to our prayers, an answer comes that appears to be in violation of laws of nature as we understand them, it is simply because we do not understand all of His laws nor the delightful variations of them. One could think of the analogy of the great symphony composer who at all times keeps you aware of a dominant theme, but who joyfully surprises you with nuances and variations stemming from that theme. None of them violate the central motif, but they give expressions that you could not possibly have conceived. What we call a "miracle" from our standpoint as human beings is simply a "mercy" from God's side. When we consider what man has done in the control of nature, it ought not to be difficult to be open to the possibilities of God.

It is not uncommon to run into people, both non-Christian and Christian, who would like to have scientific proof that prayer is effectual. Even considering the psychic experiments of Dr. Rhine of Duke University, the experiments of the effect of prayer upon plant life, the measuring of field forces in the laying on of hands, the proof of prayer is not ultimately within the field of science. Litmus paper cannot by changes of color prove prayer to a skeptic. Nor can one expect to see its effects in a microscope, or on charts of various controls. The effects of the love made available when one person prays for another are immeasurable. Who can test the courage that flows into a wearied heart when it is the recipient of prayer power?

The final and conclusive proof of prayer will always remain within the field of religious experience. It is not a fascinating toy to be played with by the casual unbeliever. Nor will the most intricate reasoning about prayer either prove or disprove its effects. This is not to say that prayer cannot stand all the tests of reason, but rather that it is far beyond its finite scope. It is only as we pray that we can know what prayer is and what prayer does. This is the divine experiment, not the human manipulation. One may have read every book on the subject, but if one does not turn to God in praise, love, and expectation, he will not know the meaning of prayer. Those who really practice prayer do not demand clinical proof that God listens and responds. The accumulated experience of answered prayer becomes the firm foundation upon which a life of increasing prayer is built.

7 Prayer and the Human Factor

Is it not amazing, in this world of humanistic achievement, that one of the inhibiting factors for a more confident, practicing Chruch at prayer, is the mistrust of the human factor? We are referring to members of the Body of Christ, and not to the unchurched, whom we should hardly regard as being concerned about the subject in the first place. The problem lies not so much in the pride of what humanity can do, in the eyes of some, without recourse to the supernatural. That argument is a bit dated, more in line with the philosophy of the "Manifest Destiny" of the early part of this century. Then, the optimists of humanism were quite certain that our ingenuity would soon create a Utopia out of technology and education. Since then, the mounting evidence of human perversity, as measured in two world wars, intermittent large-scale violence, Jewish pogroms, racial bitterness, political corruption, corporate greed, and personal depravity, has given birth to a different objection.

As might be expected, that objection lies within that obvious human fallibility and finitude which is all too apparent even without being a student of the mysteries of sin and evil. How can prayer be of value when such beings are doing the praying? Why should such a being have the wisdom to pray for the true needs of another person? Doesn't God understand these needs in a pure sense that would make our befogged requests ridiculously innaccurate? Then, again, what right do people, who scarcely know the meaning of real inner perfection, have to ask for the redemption of another person? Would we not be simply presuming upon their course of life and violating their freedom of choice? These objections suggest that it would be better to leave other human beings alone and leave the whole task up to God without the pretensions of our imperfect prayers.

Such a common opinion ignores the fervent request of our Lord Jesus Christ that we should ask, seek, and knock; and it abandons all wonderment as to why He should be so insistent that we be people of prayer if it is to no avail. More, then, needs to be said about the theology of "asking." It has much to do with the manner of creation that we are, and with the relationship between a personal God and a child whose most natural recourse is to communicate with his father.

When we pray we are not asking God to violate the freedom or the highest good of ourselves or others. We are simply asking Him to give them new freedoms of choice, new possibilities of life, that they had not held forth as possibilities. This certainly does not violate freedom, for when these opportunities are placed before them by our prayers, they still hold the veto of personal choice. This may be a large part of the phenomenon of "unanswered prayer." It is not unanswered prayer; it is rejected prayer. This means, as someone so colloquially expressed it, that we have "the freedom to flop" if that's what we will. Part of the paradox of God's love for us is that He will not even force us to accept His goodness.

An illustration of this is the visit of the rich young ruler with Jesus. He came asking what he had to do in order to have eternal life. It was a prayer, a direct asking of the Lord.

Jesus answered his request just as directly. He told him that if he would have eternal life he should sell all he had, give the money to the poor, and come and follow Him. The young man asked for the secret of life and the answer was marvellously given in the offer of personal fellowship with the Lord. He even added the key to his inability to find life, his enslavement to the perishing goods of this world. However, the young man went away dejectedly, refusing the very answer which he had sought, because he would not give up his goods. This, then, was the rejection of an answered prayer. God will not force us to choose the better way.

However, much has still been accomplished when we pray, even considering such possibilities of rejection. The way of redemption is placed before that soul for joyful acceptance. The treasures of God have been laid open to him. The instability of evil cannot be overstressed either. The forces of evil to which man clings are made up of unstable material for they are not of God. Therefore, it is when, by the channeling of our prayers, the way of God is placed upon the scales that instability becomes precipitous. The life of the prayed-for person is therefore much more easily tipped God's way than that of the person for whom no prayer is offered. Once I heard a friend say to a person who was just discovering the possibilities of prayer, "Now you are standing on the side of a slippery ditch, and it's only a matter of time until you go all the way in."

Granting that no violation of the freedom of one imperfect human being is violated by the prayers of another imperfect human being, it still remains to the skeptic to wonder about our human limitations of will and judgment. How can we presume to know what is best for ourselves or for another person?

This is where the concept of the Praying Church becomes so important. As members of the Body of Christ we do not pray as isolated dilettantes of spirituality. We are rightly suspicious of the prayer life of those who, though separated from the Church, make large majestic claims for their prayer prowess. This includes those who, functioning on their own, claim that large doses of supernatural power emanate from them. One quite instinctively shies from those who presume to tell you what your needs are and how they are personally equipped to answer them. Be wary of those private practitioners who see no necessity for the Church but who are constantly overflowing with spiritual revelation. They, indeed, can become authoritarian and manipulative.

When we offer our prayers within the framework of the Christian community, it is quite a different matter. We are not simply praying to Christ, we are praying with Him. Our prayers become sifted and purified by His presence. There is even the conscious thought, "What would Christ do in this circumstance?" There is also the fellowship to which we can go with our prayers for counsel and refinement. In the Body of Christ we pray as those who are informed by His love and the love that is evoked by our neighbor's needs.

There is another dimension to the efficacy of prayers offered within the framework of the Church. It is contained within two profound portions of Scripture. The first is that passage from Luke 11:1–13 in which the disciples ask Jesus to teach them to pray. It leads into the story of the importunate friend who insists that his neighbor arise at night and provide food so that he can feed his guest. It ends with this verse: "If you then, who are evil, know how to give good gifts to your children, how much more will the heavenly Father give the Holy Spirit to those who ask him!" There is the prior acknowledgment here of our human imperfection. In spite of this, we may ask of our finite brother and he can provide help for us. It follows that in our asking of God, even though our asking may be imperfect, we should expect our heavenly Father to respond infinitely better than our human brother. The best gift which a father can offer a child is his life of holiness. This, in unmatchable degree, is what God offers us in the gift of the Holy Spirit.

This suggests to us the meaning of another passage found in Romans 8:14f. "For all who are led by the Spirit of God are sons of God. . . . When we cry 'Abba! Father!' it is the Spirit himself bearing witness with our spirit that we are children of God." Moving ahead to verse 26 we find a key to the validity of even our imperfect prayers, "Likewise the Spirit helps us in our weakness; for we do not know how to pray as we ought, but *the Spirit himself intercedes for us* with sighs too deep for words. And he who searches the hearts of men knows what is the mind of the Spirit, because the Spirit intercedes for the saints according to the will of God."

This means that our prayers, though they may be lacking (as were those of the father who said, "I believe, help my unbelief"), are honored as being offered up within His beloved Body out of the fellowship of those who are being redeemed and sanctified. The Holy Spirit, by whom we are bound together in baptism, sanctifies our prayers just as He sanctifies our lives. A divine corrective is given to our prayers. They are still our prayers, but they have been subjected to the same redemptive process as when the offering of our sinful self is presented by Christ, justified by His presence. Our words become translated into that which is more than words, the perfect will of God. "The Spirit himself intercedes for us with sighs too deep for words . . . the Spirit intercedes for the saints according to the will of God."

After this there are still those who would wonder why God uses our prayers at all. Why should the almighty and holy God listen and respond to the prayers of small, weak, and sinful men? Man is more likely to humble himself in the face of nature than in the sight of God. He will stand before the Grand Canyon, viewing its breathtaking depth, its broad expanse, its spectacular shadows and colorations, and declare: "How insignificant we are in comparison to this vastness!" Or he will stand on the prairie and look up at the mighty canopy of stars, suns and moons beyond numbering, galaxies light years away, and say: "How can man pretend to be of any importance when he is but a speck of dust in this whole universe?" It is not difficult to illustrate our smallness and from that deduce that we are close to nothing in significance. We, therefore, should not presume to speak to God on any matter. The psalmist, however, saw it all another way:

> O Lord, our Lord, how majestic is thy name
>   in all the earth!
> Thou whose glory above the heavens is chanted
>   by the mouths of babes and infants,
> thou hast founded a bulwark because of thy foes,
>   to still the enemy and the avenger.
> When I look at thy heavens, the work of thy fingers,
>   the moon and the stars which thou hast established;
> what is man that thou art mindful of him,
>   and the son of man that thou dost care for him?
> Yet thou hast made him little less than God,
>   and dost crown him with glory and honor.
> Thou hast given him dominion over the works of
> thy hands;
>   thou hast put all things under his feet,
> all sheep and oxen,
>   and also the beasts of the field,
> the birds of the air, and the fish of the sea,
>   whatever passes along the paths of the sea,
> O, Lord, our Lord,
>   how majestic is thy name
> in all the earth! (Ps. 8).

As the Praying Church we are to understand that we are precious to God. The earth and the stars were made for the use of humanity. Though awesome to us, they are collectively of less importance to God than one human soul. The stars and the canyons have no soul; the stars shine dumbly upon the glory of mankind, the canyons gape blindly before the wonder of the human spirit. God has even created us in His own image and has bestowed His blessing upon us. We are given further insight into this uniqueness with the New Testament revelation that in Christ the human being becomes the temple of the Holy Spirit, a sanctuary, a holy place, the place of prayer. All of this is true in spite of our sinfulness. The very potentiality for sin becomes the paradoxical proof of our uniqueness in creation. Such free will bespeaks a great order of being. Something incapable of such choices would be of a lower order.

This also strongly suggests another way of looking at humanity's status as far as being a creature to whom God would lend a listening ear. In our very sinfulness God has shown what kind of God He is, a God of love, a God of nearness. In emphasizing man's frail insignificance, there has usually been the picture of a transcendent God, majestic and far-removed. This gives us a clue to the reluctance of the transcendentalists of the last century to be engaged in displays of piety. They would rather trust their own brains to work out life's problems, because they looked upon God as one who, having created the universe, set it loose in endless space, leaving man to his own devices.

However, this is not the story of the New Testament. Here we encounter a God who in Jesus Christ becomes very near because of His relentless love for us. We find the disarming picture of a Savior who is approachable by tax collectors, lepers, harlots, children, aristocrats, and peasants. He does not have to be persuaded to attend to their needs but volunteers to come among them, seeking out the lowest and the least.

This brings us to a crucial part of this discussion about the seeming ridiculousness, to some, of God's willingness to listen to human beings before acting in certain situations. It can be couched in this question: "If God loves us in the way He has revealed in the coming of Jesus Christ, will He not also listen to us?"

An everyday experience of those parents who are at the stage of raising babies illustrates the answer to this question. In the middle of the night the parents hear the cry of their baby. At first it is a tentative cry, mother and father breathe sighs of relief hoping to sink back into the deep sleep out of which they have come. But then a few more resolute cries come forth, and the realization that the infant is working himself up into a full-blown spell of crying becomes obvious. From the point of view of the logic of the superior being, having no need of the advice of an inferior being, the parents could now reason this way, "Why should I pay attention to the cries of a baby? After all, I am much larger, more powerful, more intelligent. I could ignore those cries by using ear plugs. Besides, my reasoning tells me that the child is perfectly well since, in the past when the baby cried out, he soon settled down to sleep again. The very lustiness of the cry proves that the child is alive and well. He will not starve before morning and a little dampness will not melt him." However, parents who have the least warmth of love react in an entirely different way. Because the baby cries out in the night one or the other rises up swiftly to see what the need might be. The actual need may be great distress, but in either case love reaches out in response to a cry. If human parents will respond with love to the cry of a baby, how much more will the heavenly Father listen to the cries of His children. We repeat that observation of the psychologist: "It is impossible to distinguish between listening and loving."

We come, then, to this crucial question: Even granting God's love, is it rational to believe that He would be influenced by our prayers? Here is the simple and yet profoundly fathomless answer: Our prayers have influence upon the action of God because He wills it so! He wills that we should bear this responsibility. It is part of His plan for our relationship with Him. He has willed that we should be coworkers with Him, and that we should have an opportunity to join in His plan of redemption. We may have the assurance that the Father pays heed to our prayers because it is His forthright will to do so. His willingness to act in response to our requests is a sign of His great love for us. We have, therefore, greater responsibility in our spiritual lives than many have supposed. He who gave us dominion on the earth had far greater designs for us than that we should domesticate cattle and discover minerals. He also gives us sway in the spiritual world to the extent that certain things will not happen unless we ask for them. There would be no meaning to the observation that a loving God is one who responds to mankind if that did not include his prayers. God does not impair Himself when He yields to our seeking and knocking and asking. He simply shows a greater love than a God who would have bypassed man in all of his activities.

While this says much about man's high stature it also impresses us with a greater weight of responsibility as the Praying Church. We can no longer use such bland statements as this as an excuse for an absence of a discipline of prayer: "We needn't pray, because God already knows what is best for us." We need to acknowledge that God has judged that "what is best for us" is that we be a praying people. We cannot develop spiritually without conscious, active, daily communication with Him on all matters of life. In reality, our prayers play a part in the divine plan for the redemption of the world.

He shows us that earnest prayer creates new situations which otherwise would not have come into existence. When we pray, attitudes change, particularly our own. Interests and talents are directed in new creative ways. New channels are opened up for the flow of divine action. New spiritual forces are released. We might in our imagination visualize a great reservoir of God's power and love which lies above us. Its resources are there for the asking but no person is coerced to partake of them. However, each praying person penetrates that reservoir with a pipeline that flows from that source through himself. If the world is not flooded by God's love, it is not because that love is not available. It is because He is calling for more faithful people to be channels of His grace. Then there would be a flood rather than a trickle.

It is not surprising that God would work His plan of redemption through the prayer-response of His faithful people, for it is the way He has worked throughout history. He chose a nation of people, Israel, to become the bearers of His earlier revelations—though theoretically He could have done it without them. Some might have wondered why He did not select another nation, one more intellectual perhaps. They would repeat that doggerel, "How odd of God to choose the Jews." And yet He did so, and much of this choice lies in that they were a nation of prayer, a meditating people. It was through such people that He planned to flow and act. This then became a key teaching of the New Covenant in which Jesus Christ, through His apostles, prepared a praying and worshiping Church.

Other illustrations abound of how God uses man for the channeling of His life: the use of shepherds, kings, and fishermen to become His sacred writers (their writings would still bear the stamp of those personalities); the use of common elements such as bread and wine for conveyance of the Holy Communion.

If we need a reminder of how prayer changes situations, we only need to look to the cross. There Jesus hung under the most tragic circumstances. What greater evil could surround a scene than that the King of life should be taunted and tortured by the very beings He came to love? The scene could have been even more drastically darkened had the Son of God looked upon this depravity, seen it unworthy of His love, and pronounced an everlasting curse upon it. It would have seemed deserved in the eyes of pure justice. And yet He altered that horrible scene for all time by uttering one prayer, "Father, forgive them for they know not what they do." It became, instead, the revelation of the heart of God, a heart of such love that it would not be withdrawn from us even when we had done our worst. He has shown us the power of prayer to create new situations even out of those most unlikely. Whereas one person might wallow in the nightmare of a tragedy, another will lift it to God and find from it a way of salvation for many.

8 Prayer in the Valley

The conclusion of the preceding chapter leads us into an area of prayer which is vitally important to the Praying Church —the use of prayer in times of extreme difficulty. It is comparatively easy to pray when all is well. We say "comparatively," for fair weather days are also a challenge. We find in those times that, on a superficial level, life goes along without conscious recourse to prayer. Perhaps it is because we neglected prayer when all was going smoothly that the well of prayer is dry when times of crisis come. I remember the words of the old man who was converted on his death bed. When I came to baptize him he was all but gone. Then came a miraculous recovery. His new-found faith was no passing fancy. He learned to pray daily. His words of wisdom were, "If I will walk with the Lord in the sunshine, He will walk with me in the shadows."

The 84th Psalm has a poetic thought about "prayer in the valley":

> Blessed are the men whose strength is in thee,
>   in whose heart are the highways to Zion.
> As they go through the valley of Baca

they make it a place of springs,
the early rain also covers it with pools.
They go from strength to strength;
the God of gods will be seen in Zion.

The Valley of Baca, in translation, is "the vale of misery."
It is a symbol of those dark, disturbing experiences that come
in life. Everyone must pass through this valley at some time
in his life. Perhaps it is the bitter disappointment of failure
in one's work. It may be the fact of becoming an invalid; the
pain, a feeling of uselessness. Even if a person does not
encounter such valleys of misery as poverty, disappointment,
or sickness, there is always that one valley of the shadow
which no one can escape, that of death. It is hard to conceive
of anyone who does not suffer the acute loss of someone by
death. Even if he should somehow avoid this experience with
regard to others, there is inevitably the experience of his own
death.

Thus, actually, life is not a matter of escaping the Valley
of Baca, it is a matter of what spiritual equipment one carries
with him while he is passing through that valley. It is in that
inevitable journey that we discover the true quality of our
prayer life.

A common reaction of many who are passing through the
Valley of Baca is that of defeat. These are the unashamed
wailers of this world. They are like actors in a tragic melo-
drama. They stagger from room to room, clutching at their
throats, hair disheveled. They weep and moan unconsola-
bly. In their own eyes "they walk alone." They are quite
convinced that their suffering is unique and unutterably
cruel. They fail to see that there are other pilgrims passing
through the Valley of Baca who are just as badly off as they
are, or possibly worse.

They almost seem to glory in their plight. One begins to
feel that they might seek out more trouble if present miseries

were cleared away. While they are obviously a bane and a burden to all with whom they come in contact, they do not even succeed in helping themselves while passing through the Valley of Baca. They become bitter against life, against God. They curse their fate, but they are a curse unto themselves. Their trouble may have been serious, but now it is compounded. The original misery is increased and new ones have been hatched.

A different attitude while passing through the Valley of Baca is that of the stoic. He is a fatalist. He believes that everything that happens to a person is inevitable. He grits his teeth and accepts the Valley of Baca at face value, defying his fate. There is a Spartan bravado about him. He scorns the weakling who crumbles before the test. He would be embarrassed and ashamed to be seen crying, to be heard groaning.

When I spent a summer during my seminary years among American Indians I observed this quality among the children. One day a small boy of six cut his foot on a clam shell while wading in a lake. I saw the blood spurting from his foot as he rushed out of the water to the beach, but he didn't utter a sound. Then he fled into the woods alone where, if he cried, no one would hear him.

The stoic is sometimes a hero to others, but he is more often a hero in his own image. His theme might be that of the poem *Invictus* by Henley:

> I am the master of my fate;
> I am the captain of my soul.

The stoic helps himself, at least for a time, while passing through the Valley of Baca, but he is no help to others who are passing through. There is no cheer for others; just a grim set of the face. He exhibits an unsupportable, discouraging philosophy of life, a philosophy that leads many to apathy or insanity. If all is fate, if these valleys of Baca are written in the stars for each person, then all life is mechanical. We are but manipulated machines, pawns in the hands of a capricious tyrant world. If this philosophy were followed to its logical extreme, there would be no use trying to plan and hope for the future. Progress would be unthinkable. There would be no such thing as divine goodness, mercy, or wisdom working out a benevolent purpose, but only blind, stupid maniacal forces. The stoic is eventually a tragedy to himself.

This leads us to the way of prayer, the Christian way of passing through the Valley of Baca. Somehow, by prayer, he not only finds strength enough for his own journey but he has an overflow to share with others passing the same way. The wailer helps no one, not even himself. The stoic helps himself, but no one else. But the praying person, being in Christ, passes through the Valley of Baca making it a spring. He finds refreshment and rest for himself and for other pilgrims on this way.

In Bunyan's great allegory, *Pilgrim's Progress,* there is the episode where Christian is passing through the Valley of the Shadow of Death. Bunyan knew the meaning of dealing with misery in his own life, a life filled with prayer.

"When Christian had traveled in this disconsolate condition some considerable time, he thought he heard the voice of a man going before him, saying, 'Though I walk through the Valley of the Shadow of Death I will fear no ill, for thou art with me.' " Then he was glad and for this reason: even though he was walking in darkness, from the voice of the man ahead of him he knew that he was not alone in his experience—other members of Christ had to pass through this same valley. He was glad also because obviously the man ahead was being upheld by God. He too, therefore, could expect to be upheld by God as he passed through the valley —"Thou art with me." He was glad also because he would soon overtake others passing through the valley. Then he could help them on their way and they could help him—the great fellowship of the Praying Church. Passing through the Valley of Baca he had made it a spring. Christian was actually richer spiritually for having gone through the experience.

Regarding "prayer in the valley," some of our most critical journeys are through the valley of guilt, the valley of the dark night of the soul, and the valley of death. How does the person of prayer go through them?

How can one escape the valley of guilt? On the one hand, it may seem odd that a Christian has to go through this valley. On the other hand, the Christian has been more sensitized to the evil in his own life than the modern conscienceless pagan. While he is getting closer to Christ, he is also becoming more acutely aware of the great gap between what He is and what he ought to be—between the "is" and the "ought." People who have newly become Christians have often remarked to me with some wistfulness that they were less troubled inwardly when they were living a selfish secular life. I am quick to point out to them that this is actually an encouraging sign; it means that their souls are really encountering God. There is an analogy with that of the person who has become completely lazy and inactive physically. When he realizes that, for the good of his health, he must begin exercising again, he finds it painful. Unused muscles have aches and pains for a long time. But those very pains are a sign of an improving condition.

This does not mean that attacks of guilt are joyful to experience. They require a great amount of prayer. Prayer leads us eventually to the only way out of this valley. One does not have to endure inner torture to the end of his days in masochistic justice for his deeds. One is not required to go through a prescribed period of self-flagellation until he comes out, gaunt and shriven, having beaten the evil out of himself. In prayer we are led forward to the only real answer to the deathly experience of guilt; that is the life of Christ. His answer is so remarkably simple and to the point—it is sheer, blanket forgiveness!

Sometimes, in our exasperation over our feelings, we have a hard time accepting the truth that we are forgiven that very moment. Surely we shall have to wait until next week, until we have endured more hours of torture. It is a healing miracle of Christ as He places His hands over us and says, "Thy sins be forgiven thee." It is transmitted through prayer; sometimes in the small absolving group, and often in the Gathered Church. While passing through the valley you find the spring.

Then there is the valley of the dark night of the soul. It is not the same as the valley of guilt. It can come to one who has known Christ and His forgiveness for a long time. It can come to one who has gladly accepted a disciplined life of faithfulness. Perhaps it was just a week ago that one had been on the heights of the Spirit, living close to the Lord in rarefied air. Now, suddenly, the lights seem to go out in the soul. Prayers seem to rise no higher than the ceiling and then fall dead at our feet. We seem alienated not only from the sight of God but from people around us. Our very taste buds disappear. There is a dry nothingness within that takes the color out of the sky and the trees. A gray world takes over.

What then? Is Christ gone? Has He left us? Shall we curl up and die with a lost whimper of loneliness? It is then more than ever that continuing prayer has meaning. When the dark night of the soul comes, prayer has its greatest season. This is truly the prayer of faith rather than of sight, "the substance of things hoped for; the evidence of things unseen." Here is where the discipline of the spiritual life carries us along; to keep praying regularly even though there is no answer except "Keep on praying." It is a time to keep worshiping Christ in the Gathered Church in the midst of those who still see the light. It is the great time for the quiet company of the Apostolic Group who will pray for you and with you. It is a time to thank Him who, though unseen, walks before you, making a way through a maze you cannot see.

Though darkness has come, progress along the way has not ceased; it is as dark near the last turn in a tunnel as it was in the middle, but the light will soon be seen. The only defeat for the man of prayer is to stop doing those things which were valid in the days of light, thereby losing hold of the hand of Him who is still there, the Good Shepherd. "Thou art with me; even now!" No one who has kept himself in faith and prayer in the night season has been deserted by Christ. When he has come through he has found himself with a more mature and enduring faith in which the valleys will be further apart and shorter. And a powerful witness has been made to those around us. While passing through the Valley of Baca we have made it a spring.

Yet to come is the valley of death. Everybody dies. Some seem to die too soon. We call them tragedies. Others seem to die too late. They are like the person Martin Luther King said he would become if he retired from the scenes of danger he had chosen. He could go off into a safe place and live to the age of eighty-six, but when he got to that age he would look back and realize that he had really died at the age of thirty-six only he hadn't known it.

Death has become the prevailing theme of all modern thought because so many do not know how to handle it. In our literary world, where any four-letter word is permissible, "death" is the most obscene word. It is the grim theme of modern painting. It is the somber specter of our novels and poetry. Behind the reckless thrill-seeking of so many of our time lies a shriek of the fear of ultimate extinction. It is at the heart of the youth cultists who, by aping the mannerisms and styles of the young, hope to put a magic spell upon the aging process. It is also seen in our vast materialism, which wants everything for this fleeting life because of the panicky thought that "this is all there is."

How will we react to death? We can cry and grieve for others who die. It isn't wrong to do so, but for many it becomes a way of life. Or we can try everything available to blot out the thought of our own certain death. But what else can we do? We can call out to the Good Shepherd in our prayers, and He will hear us. He will come to us and bring us to terms with the total reality of the life we are called by Him to love—both in respect to the death of others and to our own. We are nothing if we are not the people of the Resurrection. This gives us a quality of life which no other people have. In prayer we are in constant touch with the Risen One.

Death is not loss for the man of Christ. We cannot lose what Christ does not lose; namely our life, which is in His keeping. We are the people of the Resurrection. This is essentially what the spiritual life is—to be the Easter people. It is not a doctrine but a state of constant being. One could live in the regret of yesterday, but this is to live in the era of real death, for those days are gone forever. One could live in the dread or dream of tomorrow, but this is made of stuff that is even less than air. The spiritual life, which is real life, is to meet every immediate moment, every circumstance as it arrives at our heartbeat and consciousness under the Lordship of Jesus Christ. Then, when the last heartbeat comes, we shall have walked so long with, and so close to our divine companion that we shall not even notice for a moment that we have walked right into the next world.

In other words, the praying Christian does not wait for life —he lives now in the God-given way of unceasing communion. He does not wait until family problems are solved, a new level of opportunity has been presented, the present suffering is past, or until he gets more intelligent. It is now that our life in Christ deals with all these things as they come and redeems them. Prayer in the valley discovers the hidden springs.

Psalm 84 goes on to an even more fulfilling climax. Once the praying companion of Christ has made a spring in the desert valley, a wonderful thing happens from that day forward. "The rain also fills the pools." God keeps right on supplying that wellspring until it flows over and becomes a river. The power of God sanctifies our suffering so that a stream flows out to innumerable lives. "They go from strength to strength, every one of them appears before God." A hymn-verse has been inspired from Bunyan's *Pilgrim's Progress.*

> He who would valiant be gainst all disaster
> Let him in constancy follow the Master.
> There's no discouragement shall
>   make him once relent
> His first avowed intent to be a pilgrim.

9 Prayer as God's Commission

In a certain cartoon, a mother is looking at a strange puzzle in a toy store while searching for a gift for her child. The clerk behind the counter offers this explanation, "It's an educational toy, Ma'am, to help your child adjust to today's world. Any way you put it together is wrong."

This is the story of our secularized society. The secular society lives without reference to God. A society without God has no meaning. "Any way you put it together is wrong."

We may too quickly assume that only agnostics or atheists have succumbed to the secular drift. If this were true, we would have no need for this chapter because the chances are very slim that any such people will pick up this book. Our chief concern here is over the large number of Church members who have been absorbed by secularism without resisting. They have been found weak and nerveless in the face of devastating forces of spiritual erosion. Yes, they still accept certain expressions of morality and the pomp and dignity of an occasional service of worship, but without realizing it they reject the sacred view of life. This is a view which sets all earthly issues within the context of the eternal. One that sees all things here in terms of God's continual rule and earth's transitoriness. It is a view that sees that the Church is Christ's, not ours; the world is His, not ours. It sees with utter clarity that without Him we are nothing.

To counteract this secular slippage in the Church we have begun to engage in "renewal." Renewal has become one of the watchwords of today's Church. If we aren't careful, it could become a catchword. We have seen strong Christian words washed away by the flood of jargon and gimmickry that swiftly surrounds them once they are popularized. One such word is "mission." How quickly it is forgotten that it has its life and meaning in the divine commission. As a popularized concept it meant everything from social reconstruction (though this may be a by-product of Christ's mission) to supplying guns for revolutionaries. One could attend entire conferences on the mission of the Church without hearing mention of the Christian Gospel. A similar thing happened to the word "relevance." By the time relevance became a cult of aping all the "in" things of our age, it was forgotten that it is only God who makes anything relevant.

Thus, it is important to emphasize that renewal is not the work of men trying to give the Church a new look. Many churches thought renewal would come if only they would jazz up their services or put theology into today's jargon. Others thought that the new morality would renew the Church by making it more attractive to the sophisticates of our time. Still others thought renewal would come by adopting the methods of sociology, psychology, and industrial advanced planning techniques. The results of all these efforts have been disappointing in terms of renewal of the Church. Renewal has not come by these means because they have been man-centered attempts. In many cases the Church was more deeply buried in secularism than before.

Now the rediscovery is being made that renewal comes only with a focus upon the living Christ and the coming of the Holy Spirit into the Church. After all, the basic problem of the world is spiritual, and therefore the basic answer must be spiritual. The terrible problems of injustice, racism, hunger, and ignorance are symptoms of the most basic problem of mankind, which is alienation from God.

If renewal is to come, it must come to the Church and through the Church. Government is necessary, but in spite of its best efforts it cannot produce a redeemed humanity. Education is desirable because ignorance is a blight, but the highest learning of our universities cannot turn man from self-centeredness. Money is power, but the distribution of wealth has never been a guarantee of a good life.

If renewal comes through focus upon the living Christ, it must come through His Church. The Church is the extension of the Incarnation, the fellowship of the Holy Spirit. But as we say this, we realize that the Church is made up of people like us. If renewal is to come in any way that involves my life, it will have to begin in me. I cannot ask for renewal of the world, of humanity, of the Church if I am not willing to be renewed myself.

In order to do this, I must be in a constant state of surrender and conversion. This is what prayer is. St. Paul says, "The outer man is decaying but the inner man is being renewed each day" (2 Cor. 4:16). A renewed Chruch is a Praying Church. It is one which speaks and acts for God, but we cannot speak for God unless we first speak with Him. We cannot act for God unless we first know what He would have us do through our immediate confrontation with Him. We can do nothing without the power of His Holy Spirit.

Therefore, if we are to be a renewed Church, we are called to be a Praying Church. There can be no other kind of Church. Every gathering for worship is to be the means whereby Christ breaks through into our lives, into His world.

We need, in light of this, to look upon prayer as God's commission to His Church. It is not an optional exercise of certain pious folks. The commission is for all members. The main job of the parish church is the inculcation of the spiritual life. We have other works to do, but they all are inspired and empowered by our communion with the Lord of the Church. Without prayer the Church becomes a stale and dying humanitarian agency. Therefore, the focus upon prayer is paramount, fundamental, and central. It spells the life or death of the Church.

Prayer is not our activity but God's action. Activism is too often "doing our thing." We have responded to the stimuli of the world by supposing that if we are in motion we are doing something worth-while. The slogan says: "Don't just stand there, do something." The time has come for a rewording of this, "Don't just do something, stand there". Stand still in the presence of God. Know Him. Be filled by Him. Then be commissioned by Him. Yes, God wants us to act, but He wants it to be like the Acts of the Apostles, Spirit-filled and Spirit-led.

Much of our absorption in uninspired secular activism has resulted in enervating wheel-spinning. The rustic humor of the following Northern Minnesota tale is a parable of this. Spring thaws find the roads of that north country an impassable quagmire. "Mud vacation" is decreed for school children because they cannot make their way to the schoolhouse. On one of these days a man came to a low spot on the road. It was a lake of mud at least a hundred feet wide. At a short distance from the edge he saw what appeared to be a floating hat. Reaching out with a stick, he retrieved it. He was startled to see that the dome of a man's head was underneath it. Unbelievably, although only the top showed, it was moving slightly. There was life! He shouted to the owner of the head, "Can I help you?" The reply came bubbling up from the mud, "No, I'll be all right as long as my horse doesn't slip." Need we belabor the point? It speaks of the futile bravado of an activism that is going nowhere but insists it is OK.

The work of the Christian is the fruit of the Spirit. Some years ago I had the privilege of sitting for a few days at the feet of one of the greatest missionaries of the twentieth century, E. Stanley Jones. He told the story of his first year in India. He had gone there as a young minister full of anticipation of what he would soon accomplish there. After a year had gone by he was quite disillusioned. He had made no inroads upon the non-Christians. He had worked and strained long hours for converts to no avail. His self-convincing seminary argumentations had fallen on deaf ears. In short, he felt like a failure.

In this state of depression he lay beneath a fruit tree wondering what he would do next. He was exhausted and discouraged, and he felt he should resign and return to America. But God wasn't through with him yet. Seemingly, God had His opportunity as soon as Stanley slowed down enough to be open to His voice. Indeed, He then spoke to him through the fruit tree. Within himself Stanley heard God say, "Observe this tree, it bears fruit effortlessly." This was all he heard, but it was enough. Stanley Jones realized that he had been trying to do everything by his own effort and, though he spoke of God, he was not going to the roots of faith through constant prayer. The tree did not strain or groan in the production of fruit. It simply sent down its roots and then, silently, beautifully, nourishingly, the fruit appeared. E. Stanley Jones went on to be one of the most successful missionaries of our time among the most intellectual caste of Indians, the Brahmins.

God commissions us to prayer. How does this commission come to us? It comes principally through the example of the praying Christ. His whole earthly ministry was shot through with prayer. He and His disciples did nothing without prayer. As He began this ministry, He spent forty days in the wilderness in meditation, seeking the Father's direction for the messianic mission. During that mission He was constantly taking time to go up into the hills to pray, sometimes alone, sometimes with His disciples. He would rise up early in the morning before the sun came up to pray for the Father's will and presence throughout the day. He would pray over the sick and the troubled.

It dispels any theory that frequent or lengthy prayer is for those who have little else to do. Think of it, in three years' time He had to proclaim His kingdom, instruct His apostles, found the Church, and save the world. In terms of the common reaction of our times to such a regimen, one would have thought that He would be frantically dashing off in all directions at once, feverishly running from one organizational meeting to another, nervously aware of deadlines. And yet, amazingly, He *walked* through His ministry.

He walked so that the sick could catch up to Him. Even the weakened woman who had been hemorrhaging for so long was able to touch the hem of His garment. He could stop to take the little children into His arms. The disciples, though they sensed only a part of His mission, felt much more pressed for time and tried to keep the children from bothering Him. But he had time for them. As He walked, people of all sorts and conditions would sidle up to Him. He had time to eat with the tax collector, to sit and have His feet washed by a forgiven woman.

Our Lord was able to walk through His ministry without haste, but without ceasing, because He was constantly in communion with the Father. Our own commission of prayer comes from His life of prayer. If the Son of God found it necessary to lead a life saturated with prayer, how much more necessary it is for us. For me, when the question "Why should we pray?" is asked, it becomes an all-encompassing answer to say, "Because Jesus did." We need no greater rationale or argument for prayer than this. It becomes in itself our commission of prayer.

The headline, "Personal Prayer Making Strong Comeback

in U.S.," appeared in a large Minnesota newspaper. The
by-line had the name of George W. Cornell, religion writer
for the Associated Press. The following excerpts speak of a
renewed confirmation of the prayer commission.

> After a period of decline, prayer is regarded by many reli-
> gious authorities as now making a strong comeback. An
> "inward turn," the Rev. W. Norris Clarke, a Jesuit philoso-
> pher, calls it. It is a "turn back to contemplation as to the
> living roots of truly fruitful action," he adds. "This is what
> we find happening all around us today."
>
> "People all about us are hungry for dimensions of mystery,
> for experiences of the spirit," says the Rev. Dr. C. F. Allison.
> "In the past decade, as technology swelled and religious
> forces concentrated mainly on operational reforms, theologi-
> cal inquiry and widespread action for social justice, many
> church scholars cited a dwindling of past disciplines of
> prayer. But now they see a reviving awareness of the need for
> inner consciousness and prayer, a turning to devotional re-
> sources to firm up the religious basis for action in the world."

10 How to Succeed in Prayer

When one is counseling a person, it doesn't take long to find out what he knows about prayer. You find that there are gradations of conscious prayer awareness.

First of all, there are those who, when confronted with the question, "Have you prayed about this?" look at you as if you were a strange creature that just crawled out from under a cabbage leaf. You can see in their eyes that they are wondering "What in the world does my problem have to do with prayer?" These are people who don't pray and don't want to.

Second, you meet those who say they have prayed, but when they reveal how they have done it you realize that they are trying to bend God to their own purposes and are not concerned about God's will. These are people who pray, but only to themselves.

Third, you meet those who wistfully want to be able to pray but don't know how to begin or what to pray for. They give up because they believe that there are the sainted few who know about prayer but that the rest of humanity is doomed to its own fumbling thought processes. These are people who don't pray but who want to.

Fourth, there are those who are quite practiced in prayer,

who even have had occasion to counsel others about it, but who have lapses in communication with God. These bring painful periods of spiritual retrogression and dryness. These are people who do pray but have still more to learn about God and about themselves. In fact, even among the most dedicated people of prayer, there are few who do not find occasional identification with this gradation of prayer.

How can one succeed in prayer? Are there any guidelines that will keep us on the track? We will find that the meaning of "success" in prayer will be qualified by these very guidelines. What people are often asking for is assurance about the efficacy and validity of prayer rather than prowess.

The first and primary guideline for success in prayer is to build ones prayer life upon the solid assurance that prayer is ordained by God Himself. This was underlined in the preceding chapter, but it can be expanded in many ways. Every one who was ever close to God, who was ever mightily used by Him, was a person of prayer. He knew that prayer was the God-ordained means of communication with Him.

Mother Teresa of Calcutta takes prayer as a "given" in the Christian life. That it is ordained and validated by God is a simple assumption. Mother Teresa has been highly acclaimed for her tireless, sacrificial ministrations to wretched people who have been left to die in the streets of Calcutta. In an address in Boston she said: "We are not social workers. We are contemplatives right in the heart of the world. For we are trying to pray the work—to do it with Jesus, to do it for Jesus, and to do it to Jesus."

In commenting on her life, *Time* magazine said: "Most living saints, activists or no, of course get down on their knees and pray, some for hours a day. In the traditional concept of sainthood, in fact, prayer is an essential condition of sanctity, the key to the deeds that surround it. Most of today's saintly people would agree that the concept has not changed. 'To keep a lamp burning,' Mother Teresa told Correspondent Shepherd, 'we have to keep putting oil in it.' To build her own faith, she said, 'I had to struggle, I had to pray, I had to make sacrifices before I could say "yes" to God.' "*

In recent years, before prejudice about prayer began to fade, I found myself in certain Christian circles where I encountered the opinion that prayer was under suspicion. Now mind you, I'm not talking about associations with non-believers, with whom we may assume that the validity of prayer would be questioned. Trying to assess the reasons for this suspicion, I came up with these:

(1) There were those who felt that people ought not to pray too much. They were afraid that they would become religious fanatics if they did. This fear probably lay behind the following experience. I was working at that time with a planning committee in preparation for a prayer conference. They had asked me to present a proposed format for the three-day event. As a closing experience for the conference I had proposed a time of "participatory prayer." By the process of elimination, the committee had decided to stay upon the "safe" ground of teaching and workshops on the subject of prayer. There were several worried looks as they considered the proposal of "participatory prayer." Finally one person said, "That part of the program distrubs me. I think it's too much to expect people to engage in actual prayer." Another chimed in, "I agree. I think it will turn a lot of people off. Perhaps it would be better if we didn't mention prayer at all and called it a dialogue on better ways of communication." What came out clearly was that it would be all right to talk about prayer, but to pray in actuality was scary and leaned toward fanaticism. An answer to this will come later in the chapter.

(2) Then there were those who felt that people ought to avoid praying informally in the context of small groups.

Time, December 29, 1975, p.56

They were afraid that the laity were too ill-equipped in theology to be able to handle prayer in this way, and they were quite certain that such people would end up with gossip sessions or fall into the teachings of strange cults.

(3) There were also those who felt that prayer could no longer be defined in the traditional terms of being an act of communication with God. In these days of the secular city, prayer had to be redefined as doing good works in the community and bringing in a new social order. These latter were expressing the suspicion that prayer was a form of escapism. The actions of Mother Teresa, Schwester Selma of Jerusalem, Dom Helder Camara of Brazil, Surgeon Carl Becker of Africa, Dr. Cicely Saunders of St. Christopher's Hospital in London, Herman Gmeiner of the SOS refugee villages of Austria, and untold others, give adequate reply to that suspicion. All are deep in their prayer lives. It somewhat startled two prominent sociologists to discover, in a national survey, that people of prayer had a much more highly developed social consciousness than those who did not pray.*

The validity of prayer comes from the fact that God asks us to pray. He does not ask us to do anything that is futile. A sign of renewal in prayer is the acknowledgment that Christianity is openly and unabashedly supernatural. God is not an absentee landlord who leaves us to our own resources until He comes to collect the rent. God is sovereign over this world, and our greatest responsibility is to give Him full sway. The power of men is fatally limited, but the power of God is unlimited. He has promised to give His power to those who seek Him in prayer.

It is true, therefore, that "the meek will inherit the earth." The word "meek" has been greatly misunderstood. It has been assumed by many that it means "timid," an image of

*Cf. Thomas C. Campbell and Yoshio Fukuyama, *The Fragmented Laymen: A Study of Church Participation* (Philadelphia: Pilgrim Press, 1970).

the constantly cowering figure of Casper Milquetoast of the comic strips of the 30s. It means anything but that. The Greek word for "meek" is *praus,* which was a word used for the domestication of a wild ox. Once the ox became broken to the yoke and became obedient to the master, the animal was referred to as *"praus."* This speaks directly to the point that to succeed in prayer one needs to make the simple act of obedience in response to our Lord, who has ordained prayer and decreed that we should engage in it. The meek shall inherit the earth because they are in union with the creator of the earth by prayer.

We continue to pray over all things, large or small, because prayer is ordained by God Himself. He has asked us to pray; therefore we need not apologize for praying. Knowing that He has asked us to pray, it is our sacred responsibility (or response) to pray to Him. True, it is our joy and privilege, but we don't find this out until we have disciplined ourselves to engage in it.

The second guideline follows from the first, and that is: to succeed in prayer one must *pray*—the simplest statement one can make, and yet it is profoundly true. The only failure in prayer is to cease praying. Many people get hung up about prayer because they think of it in formalized terms. They have assumed that prayer was something you did after you had arrived at a more refined state of religious awareness. After all, you could not speak to God unless you were schooled in theology and could speak to him in words that sounded like the Collect for the Day out of the Book of Common Prayer.

Actually, at whatever point of life we find ourselves, God does not examine us upon the intricacies of doctrine. This is not to downgrade the study of sound doctrine; it is to say that God does not wait for us to be well versed in these matters before He is willing to converse with us. Nor does He care if we are able to speak to Him in the king's English. All that

He cares is that we speak to Him (in any manner we are capable of) and that we allow Him to speak to us. It is possible for one to have used the holy-sounding words for years and never to have spoken to God. It may even be that in a time of distress one will say with some resentment, "Lord I'm really angry with you about this!" and find that for the first time he has really spoken directly to God and opened up a way to Him.

The most advanced practitioners of prayer have often been the most simple in their approach to God, and as a result they pray more often. It is not a formalized exercise. It is like talking to a family friend, though not with a familiarity which presumes "chumminess" with God. It is a closeness that is based upon the witness of the Holy Spirit that we are the children of God (Rom. 8:15–16) and that we may therefore cry, "Abba! Father!" This is the same unique address which Christ used in the Garden of Gethsemane, and which can only be understood in terms of "Dad."

This means that we can converse with God at any time, at any place: while at work, driving a car, caring for a family, visiting a friend, or dealing with a sudden problem. One doesn't become a religious fanatic by conversing with God continuously. How could one possibly be too influenced by His will? A fanatic is something else; it is someone who presses twice as hard once he has lost sight of his goal.

Thus far we have looked at two guidelines to success in prayer. (1) Prayer is ordained by God and is therefore given all the validity needed for pressing confidently forward in the discipline. (2) To succeed in prayer one simply must pray. You cannot know about praying merely by talking about it, any more than your thirst can be quenched by a cup of water merely by standing beside it and discussing its virtues. You have to lift up the cup and drink of it.

There is yet a third guideline: prayer means self-offering. This, being a large subject in itself, will be dealt with in the following chapter.

11 Giving Yourself with Your Prayer

The third guideline for success in prayer: as self-offering in and through prayer. A beginning of this thought was made in Chapter Four, where we followed the journey from self-acceptance to self-offering. A primary reason that many do not find a growing prayer life is that they fail to offer themselves along with their prayer.

We have not really prayed if we have refused to let God have our lives. We are merely wishfully hoping that a benevolent being will steer things in such a way that our lives will be enriched but not disturbed. Actually, a praying person experiences quite a lot of disturbance. It often begins with the painful realization that we are withholding too much of ourselves from the will of God. We begin to discover that many idols will have to be destroyed in the process of our more complete self-surrender. We part from them reluctantly, as if they were being amputated from our body.

In World War II the pilots of our large bombers sometimes had to lighten the load of their aircraft because one of their motors was hit. They could barely limp back to their base, and the only way they could hope to make it was by throwing out all loose equipment. This was fairly easy as long as it meant tossing out impersonal things such as weaponry and seats. But when the captain ordered the removal of more personal items, such as parachutes, cameras, and souvenirs, there was serious grumbling. However, every excess pound could make the difference between life and death. Everything finally had to go in order to remain aloft. So it is with self-offering in prayer.

As we grow in the life of prayer, accepting God's will more completely, we also move toward greater consecration of ourselves. We are divinely assured that we are ultimately secure in the hands of God and that the only things to be destroyed in the process will be our idols. The dearest idol is our stubborn self-determination, and to this we can finally say, "Good riddance." We are learning that success in prayer is not to have our way but being able to say "yes" to God. If we enter into prayer with the thought that we will accept His answer only if it meets with our preconceived notion as to what it ought to be, we have prayed in vain. God's victory in us and through us, into that part of His world our lives can touch, comes when we become willing instruments in His hands.

Thus it was that Jesus prayed, "For their sake I consecrate myself, that they also may be consecrated in truth" (Jn. 17:19). This consecration made Him an offering along with His prayer. It was a consecration that led Him to Gethsemane where He prayed, "Nevertheless, not my will, but thine be done." This is the spirit of prayer which knows that the best that is possible in one situation might mean the removal of suffering, but that in another it might mean sacrifice. Whichever is the case, God's great love has been perfectly expressed and blessings will abound. Christ's prayer in Gethsemane led Him to Calvary to be a full, perfect, and complete self-offering. The more difficult "yes" was the channel of redemption for all mankind. In this whole development we find that the means by which this process was ordered was prayer.

What does this mean to us in the practicality of everyday prayer? It means, for example, that if we pray for a person who has a problem, God knows that we are willing, if need be, to be used as part of the solution. It means that when we pray for the conversion of a person, we dedicate ourselves to God on behalf of that soul to bring him into Christ's light. It means that when we pray for the strengthening of another person, we are willing to give our own strength if needed. It means that when we pray for those who are sick and suffering, we enter fully into their misery ourselves. Thus Francis of Assisi's prayers for the lepers led him to live among them to minister to their daily needs.

I, who had so often told others of this all-important aspect of prayer, was put to severe testing upon it on one particular occasion. Our son, Charles, was a junior at a private high school in Kansas City. One day he came home from school complaining of sore eyes. Before another hour had gone by he was in terrible pain. We hoped that an eyewash might help and that the inflammation would go away. However, in a short time he ran out the back door of our home in agony to see if the cold winter air would bring relief. Then, when we ran outside and looked at his eyes, we were aghast for they had turned blood red. It was quite apparent that they were burning from some terrible substance, whether from a chemical at school or a strong ingredient he was using on facial sores.

We made quick arrangements for an ophthalmologist to meet us at the emergency ward of a nearby hospital. The doctor was there almost as soon as we were. He made a careful examination of our son's eyes in a darkened room, using the latest diagnostic equipment. When he had seen them under powerful magnification, the doctor came to my wife and me with a grave look. We wish that he had spared Charles, who was sitting near us, his next words. It would have seemed gentler to explain it to him in less drastic terms.

He said, "I'm afraid your son has suffered an acute chemical burn in both eyes. In all probability, he will need corneal transplants if he is to see clearly again."

We were quite unprepared for this; it left us shaken and sick. It was heartrending to look at our son who was now sagging in complete agony of comprehension. The doctor, undoubtedly perceiving that he would suffer too much mentally by being left alone in the hospital, told us to take our son home with us and put him to bed. This we did, after he had been given a salve to relieve some of the burning pain. We were to bring him to the doctor's office the next day.

In the darkness of his third-story bedroom we knelt by Charles's bed in prayer. Then I rose up and laid my hands on his head, praying for the healing touch of the Great Physician. I stayed with him for while after that to keep him company. His pain had subsided enough that, despite the grim news of the doctor, he wanted me to help him with his calculus. It was all the more poignant to have him work out these difficult problems in his head as I read them aloud. What abilities God had given him! But now what would become of them?

He drifted off to sleep and I went down to our own bedroom on the floor below. There I knelt in prayer again. In the midst of my prayer I was led to ask the question, "Lord, what offering do I have to give for my son?" It came very clearly to me. He could have one or both of my eyes. Charles and I had such similar facial structures, such a matching of genes, that a transplant should be highly successful. All this came to me with no feeling of nobility or pride. In fact, when the offering was made I was flooded over with a sense of peace. I was able to go to bed and to sleep without the nightmares I thought I would have. I remembered how Jesus had said, "Take my yoke upon you, and learn of me; . . . and ye shall find rest unto your souls. For my yoke *is* easy, and my burden is light." Again, that yoke of obedience. Saying "yes" to God actually gives rest to your soul because in that acquiesence the warfare is over; you are at peace.

When I went up to see Charles on the following morning he was sitting up in his bed smiling. The pain was gone. Furthermore his eyes looked completely clear. Most thrilling of all—he could see! There was much giving thanks to God even as we drove with him to the doctor's office.

The ophthalmologist was amazed to see him in this condition, but he gave him a thorough eye examination. I noticed that he turned quite white as he pondered this turn of events. He was one of the top doctors in the field and was not given to making such diagnoses without sound scientific knowledge and practiced consideration. He stammered a bit as he said that our son's eyes looked quite well. However, he was determined that Charles should see another ophthalmologist that very morning, one of the experts in ophthalmology, an instructor in the Kansas Medical School. This examination verified a complete healing. The doctor detected signs of recent burns around the edges of the eyes, but he pronounced him well, with no complications or possible future problems.

That healing came in this way shows the marvelous repertoire of God's works. On the other hand, if I had been required to give of my eyes, I would have been no less convinced that God had answered my prayers.

When we turn to our Lord for the sake of others, we not only express a willingness to accept His will but we go further and offer ourselves as a channel through which His will might be done, even though it may be the way of Calvary. However, in doing so we have life, for "he who loves his own soul shall lose it; but he who forsakes himself will be saved" (Mt. 10:39).

The secret of this kind of expendability is that the one who has come this far in prayer has come to know the risen Christ. He knows that life here is meant to be given away, as He gave His life for us. Christ has provided so bountifully for His fellow workers that they can join St. Paul in the exultant expression, "For me to live is Christ, and to die is gain" (Phil. 1:21).

12 Quiet Prayer

As a friend of mine recently alliterated, "Life is full of traffic, TV, temper, tantrums, and tizzies." If you want quiet, it's hard to find in many places or styles of life. Yet, if there were quiet to be found, few would seek it. People purposely fill their lives with sound. In some homes the television runs from morning to night even if no one is concentrating on it. One of the symptoms of our spiritual dis-ease is that we hate to be alone. If we are forced to be alone, we try to fill the silence. We know of people who, when they are by themselves, spend their time calling everyone they know on the telephone. One of the ironies of the camping scene these days is that people go out to a wilderness setting to park their camper among other campers in an area of much denser population than they had left. Then, instead of going to a quiet place in the woods, they stay by their camper playing rock music as loudly as they can. When night comes, instead of sitting under the stars, they go inside where the eerie blue light of their portable TV can be seen shining out their window.

Far more serious, in the process of spiritual erosion, than physical sonar waves is the inner racket of frenetic lives. This is the all-too-familiar problem of stress in the midst of a pressurized society. People get to the point of living (or dying) on burned out spiritual energy. They use up all their reserves and then they borrow against an account into which no deposits have been made. When crisis comes they try to draw from it but nothing is there. There is emotional bankruptcy.

Many are dying while very active. Like Richard Cory, of Edward Arlington Robinson's poem, these people are often admired.

> And he was rich—yes, richer than a king—
>   And admirably schooled in every grace;
> In fine, we thought he was everything
>   To make us wish that we were in his place.
>
> So on we worked, and waited for the light,
>   and went without meat, and cursed the bread;
> And Richard Cory, one calm summer night,
>   Went home and put a bullet through his head.*

Most people who are overextending themselves do not come to such drastic ends. They simply shred apart inwardly before their time. A cemetery marker for one of the leading men of a community, who was "into everything" but who died of early exhaustion, had this chiseled error, "Here lies the Most Committeed Man We Have Known." He belonged to so many things that he was finally "clubbed" to death.

One evening as I was working late in my study at church a layman stopped by to see me. He was one of the most prominent consulting engineers in the United States. He owned his own two-engine plane, which he flew to his projects in every part of the nation. Though he was in his mid-

*"Richard Cory," in *Modern American Poetry*, ed. Louis Untermeyer (New York: Harcourt, Brace and Co., 1942).

thirties, he was already a wealthy man. He had a lovely country estate where he kept a stable of riding horses. He had an attractive family upon which he showered every luxury. In short, he was the envy of many in that area. What more could a man want? That night he sat by my desk and lowered his head into his open palms and sobbed. His shoulders shook as the tears ran through his fingers. Finally, when he could control himself enough to speak, he said, "There must be something more!" This cry, coming from a man who seemed to have everything, is the symbolic cry of modern humanity.

After an evening of counseling, I suggested to this searching soul that he try out an early morning prayer group in which men met quietly week after week. Each of the sessions, whether meeting in a home or outdoors at a park in the morning mist, began with a period of quiet prayer. There he found the "something more" for which he was searching— it was God, in the midst of the silence.

The use of quiet, of silence, of listening is essential in prayer. Just to be quiet before God, with no agenda, and to discover that in the heart of the silence there is a Presence —this is powerful prayer. There is no other way we can begin seeing all things in the light of eternity. When we become slaves to temporality we are no longer equipped to redeem time.

One of the classic ways of quiet prayer is the use of meditation. Many in our time are seeking commercialized versions of this. Though these methods are shallow and most often center upon self-realization (which is our problem-center rather than our solution), it is difficult to criticize those who make these attempts. They are simply trying to buy something which they deeply sense they need in these nerve-shattering times, a sense of peace and quiet. It may be that the Church, which has forgotten that it is commissioned to be the Praying Church, has neglected to tell these people that meditation has always been a strong Christian discipline. They have not heard that it is free to all who want it, and that it will lead them to communion with the inexhaustible resources of God, whose height, depth, width, and length surpass all knowledge.

Here is a way of meditation which I have found helpful. Meditation often uses mnemonic devices so that its steps can easily be remembered. In this case it is based upon ten "R"s. Seven of these "R"s were suggested to me by the Rt. Rev. Cuthbert Bardsley, Bishop of Coventry. However, he never gave them as steps in meditation but as categories of prayer. In each case I have adapted my own thought and experience so that I may truly say that they have become my own—my own to share.

Those who are familiar with some of the classic steps of meditation will find them barely hidden within this framework—the steps of relaxation, concentration, contemplation, affirmation, and resolution.

1. **Relax.** Relaxation is necessary for the use of quiet in prayer. In relaxation it is helpful to find a quiet place. It might mean getting up a little earlier in the morning or arriving at work before others get there. Even with these efforts we may find that noise persists around us—jet planes overhead, trucks going by, the furnace or the air conditioner going. However, the noise about which we are most concerned is the inner noise. This is where the actual techniques of relaxation come in. We need to be able to let go of our tensions, our mind-disturbing thoughts, in order to let God speak to us. Our preoccupation with our busy world becomes a barrier to spiritual communion.

Physical relaxation can be learned. After all, we are made by God to be body, mind, and spirit, so it should not be surprising that we have to deal with our body as we communicate with our creator. I find it best to be seated for relaxation. Kneeling is good for other times of prayer, but for a longer period of quiet one may become too conscious of aching knees. I concentrate upon letting the tautness out of the muscles of the neck and shoulders. Then I work into the mid-area of the body where the proverbial butterflies are wont to gather. From there I concentrate upon the relaxation of the legs, knees, ankles, feet, and toes. If this has not sufficed, I begin all over again, this time from the toes to the top of the head.

Americans have a peculiar sense of guilt about relaxation. There is something decidedly "un-American" about it. We feel we ought to be busy at all times. Three young people fromthe American Field Service program spoke at Rotary meeting about their impressions of the United States—one was from Ceylon, another from Switzerland, and the third from Argentina. Each one in turn, spoke of his admiration for this country and its friendly people, but each also spoke of the American inability to relax. Life here was much too hurried and intense for them.

2.**Realize.** This step speaks of the realization of God within our relaxed quietude. It is possible to relax almost to the point of sleep, but now has come the time to focus upon Him whose presence is at the heart of the silence.

For focus upon the realization of the presence of God I have come in the past few years to the use of the Jesus Prayer: "Lord Jesus Christ, Son of God, have mercy on me, a sinner." This prayer is found ten times within the synoptic Gospels. I use it quietly, in a repetitive way. I had difficulty in resorting to this kind of prayer because for years I had a feeling that to pray a prayer more than once at one time would be engaging in those "vain repetitions" against which Jesus warned. Now I realize that some repetitions are vain and others are not. Those that are vain are those which have the "prayer wheel" concept; that is, if one says a certain prayer often enough, one will gain merit by sheer numerical proof of piety. Those that are not vain are those which are simply used for the adoration of the Lord and the seeking of His presence. Persons who might look dimly upon repeated use of the Jesus Prayer may not realize that it is no different from the joyous habit that some have developed of saying, "Praise the Lord," many times each day. It seeks no favors; it simply acknowledges His love.

The background for this kind of praying is steeped in both the Old and New Testament traditions of devotion. The pious Jew "blessed the Lord" as many as a hundred times a day. It was considered robbery to God not to acknowledge His presence in all of life. So the Jew blessed the Lord for his cattle, the sun, the dew, the rain, his family, his friends, his food, his raiment, "for all things bright and beautiful, all creatures great and small." We see this practice of blessing the Lord (which in the Greek translation was *eucharistein,* "to thank" the Lord) in the earthly life of Jesus Christ. He also incorporates the use of repeated phrases in his example of prayer. How often he uses the word "Father." Again, we might understand the Lord's Prayer better as a series of short petitions, each a breath long. Some of these become repeated prayers by themselves—"Father," Thy kingdom come," "Thy will be done."

The Jesus Prayer, adopted from the devotions of the Greek Orthodox, takes on additional meaning for us. This prayer was used in early times by the Christian monks at Mt. Sinai. From there it was carried to the Greek Orthodox Church. Nearer to our own times, the Jesus Prayer became a strong part of the Russian Orthodox devotionalism. The power in this prayer lies in the name of Jesus. When we become Christians His name becomes ours. Now we come to a deeper understanding of certain New Testament texts such as: "Where two or three are gathered *in my name,* there am I in the midst of them" (Mt. 18:20). "If you ask anything *in my name,* I will do it" (Jn. 14:14). St. Paul refers to members of the Body of Christ as "those who in every place call on

the name of the Lord" (1 Cor. 1:2). To call on the name of
Jesus is to be in His presence. His name is more than nomen-
clature; He is with those who call upon Him.

To have Him become a part of your breathing no longer
sounds strangely mystical when we understand that our
Lord pervades our total lives—mind, body, and spirit. The
Greek Orthodox Church calls the Jesus Prayer an "aspira-
tion," a breathing. It takes the form of breathing in Christ
at every waking and sleeping moment. Here we discovered
the importance of the three biblical meanings of the Greek
word *"pneuma."* In some references *pneuma* means "the
vital principle by which the body is animated"—in other
words, "live." In the third usage, *pneuma* means "the Spirit
of God." Sometimes the reference is to the Holy Spirit
(pneuma hagion), or to the Spirit of God *(pneuma theou),* or
to the Spirit of Christ *(pneuma Christou).* Three meanings:
breath! life! Spirit!

Now the efficacy of the Jesus Prayer as a way of focusing
upon the pervading presence of God becomes apparent. *God*
is in our total *life,* so that in our very *breath* we are in Him.
We are brought back to the Creation, in which God breathes
into man and he becomes a living soul. We move to Christ's
encounter with Nicodemus, in which He tells him that if a
man is to be born anew, he must be born of the Spirit, and
that the Spirit blows where He wills and no one knows from
whence He comes or where He goes. At the time of the
Resurrection, Jesus breathes upon His disciples and they are
filled with the Holy Spirit. Then, on the Day of Pentecost,
the Holy Spirit comes with a rushing, mighty wind.

All this is in the Jesus Prayer. There have been times in
my travels, leading retreats and prayer conferences, when I
have found myself in different sleeping places each night.
Once there were thirty-six consecutive nights in which I was
in a strange place every night. It was not uncommon for me
to wake up in the middle of the night and not know where

I was. I would come out of a deep sleep with nothing but darkness around me and no clues to tell me of my location. I could remember times in the past when this had happened, and I would fight furiously to gain orientation. It could become quite frightening. Then I found myself saying the Jesus Prayer. With each saying of it, the Lord became more and more focused. Wonderfully, I knew I was in His presence. I realized that it didn't matter where I was geographically as long as I knew where I was spiritually. I was with the Lord. With that knowledge I would sink back to sleep.

3. **Release.** The step of release means that once we have realized His presence we are to leave ourselves in His hands. Here, again, we come to that growing edge of prayer, which is the act of surrender. It is commitment of as much of ourselves as we now know and understand to as much of Him as we we now know and understand. In quiet prayer we do this without pressure or anxiety. We have already conceded that God is love. Therefore, as we release ourselves to His will, we are not cowering before Him waiting for the first blow to fall upon us. Whatever He wills for us comes out of His love.

There is a wholesomeness about this kind of release. It stands squarely upon the Good News that by faith in His grace we are loved as we are—incomplete. And yet it does not leave us there, because in this step we find that there is continually more that God reveals about our selves. Therefore, there comes a greater understanding of what more we need to surrender to Him.

4. **Rely.** In our time of quiet we are now led from release to reliance. This is a natural step. We would not release our lives to someone upon whom we did not rely. Another word we might use is "trust." In some ways this is a more descriptive word for the meaning of "faith" than any other. Many are apt to think of faith in terms of a body of doctrine—"the faith." More than an assent to certain religious teachings,

what faith means is trust in a personal God, the God who is found to be trustworthy in the revelation of Jesus Christ.

Thus one simple word in the Apostle's Creed takes on great significance. That word is "in." "I believe *in* God the Father Almighty" . . . *"in* Jesus Christ our Lord" . . . *"in* the Holy Spirit." We are not simply saying, "I believe that there is a triune God." This would be little more than if I were to say, "I believe that I have a neighbor named Smith." You acknowledge Smith's existence but you do not imply any relationship to him. If you were to say, "I believe *in* my neighbor, Smith," it speaks a volume. You would aid him in time of need, you would trust him for help, you would vote for him if he ran for office. So when we say "I believe *in* God," we are speaking of a personal relationship of trust.

There was a time in my life when I came to learn the terms of such reliance. Over a period of eighteen months an unusual number of critical situations came into our lives. It began when my wife was struck from behind as she was sitting still in our car waiting to make a turn. It was a terrible accident, which put her in the hospital for twenty-one days and left her with painful injuries that would necessitate hospitalization and therapy for more than three years afterward. Not two weeks later, we learned that my mother-in-law had cancer. She was to linger painfully with this for eighteen months. My wife, despite her own pain, was required to be with her months at a time. This was cause for loneliness as well as deep concern. Then her mother died. We knew she was with the Lord, and yet the natural feeling of loss was there. Two weeks later my father, who we thought was doing quite well, suddenly died. We stood by his bed after rushing several hundred miles through the night to the hospital where he lay. There, just as the sun rose, he breathed his last breath in this world. I was to experience the pangs of the removal of a parent. One does not really know the meaning of this as one consoles another unless one has experienced it oneself. A week later my grieving mother came to stay with us. Within a few days she fell and, upon examination, it was discovered she had cancer. She would have a long series of cobalt treatments.

About this time I can clearly recall driving down the streets of the city on my way to the parish office. So many things had happened so suddenly and unceasingly that I found myself complaining to the Lord. I had found good precedent for this in the psalmists. I said "Lord, it seems too much. Before I can adjust to one thing, another comes along. You know I have a large parish to deal with, and hundreds of people have problems. How am I to go among them smiling with the world constantly falling apart? Lord, I have come to the point of giving up on this world. You'll have to take care of things because I can't."

Before another thought could come, God spoke to me. It was not audible, but it came to me inwardly, very clearly, "If all you have left is my love, it is enough." As I heard this, I was filled to the brim with peace. God had not promised that anything would be stationary or permanent in this world. When all else is gone, and some day it will be, His love will still be there. If His love is sufficient in the end, it is also sufficient now. I can rely on Him through all the passing things of life. How often, in times of evidence of the transitoriness of the world, I have come back to this reliance.

In the following chapter we shall continue the ten steps of meditation, from "Read" to "Renew."

13 From Read to Renew

The Christian way of meditation can be practiced by anyone who is willing to make holy use of silence. It is not the property of a spiritual elite who harbor secret practices. It is not necessary to be initiated into certain formulas to be able to meditate. Mainly, it is to be quiet in His presence; "to be still and know He is God." What is offered here is a suggested way of meditation that may be used by anyone as it fits his devotional life, adding or subtracting as he sees it fitting into what he discovers to be God's way of prayer for him at this time of his life. Fortunately there are no laws to decree the exact details of ones walk with God. The Spirit continues to blow where He wills within the unique context of every soul.

With this in mind, we continue to examine these stages of meditation.

5.**Read.** One of the great traditions of Christian meditation is the practice of prayerful reading. This is not the same as reading a textbook in preparation for a test. If it is the Bible that is being read, and it usually is, it is not a studious breakdown of dating, authorship, sources, and historicity. Exegesis has its rightful place, but not here.

The purpose of reading the Bible for meditation is to allow

God to speak to you through the Scriptures. It is more in the spirit of the following true story of a remote tribe in South America. The Bible was being translated into the language of the tribe chapter by chapter by an American linguist. Each week a messenger would bring them a portion of the translation through the jungle trails from a remote post office. One week the portion was not delivered, and there was great concern within the village. So they sent one of their leaders on the long trek to the post office, a day's journey. At the post office window he explained his mission, saying, "We need to know what God has to say to us this week. You see, that's us in those words."

"That's us" is a significant way of looking at the use of the Bible in meditation. We are called upon to use our God-given imagination in order to enter into the Bible stories and to become a part of them. Contained in the word "imaging" is "image." Many meditators speak of "imagining" yourself into the scriptural narratives. You are there; the Lord is speaking to you within those contexts.

My first understanding of this way in which the Holy Spirit illuminates the reading of the Bible came when I was still in college. Each evening a small group of us students would meet in a room in the dormitory for prayer and Bible study. It was an important experience in my life because out of it was to come my call to the ministry. Evening after evening I discovered that everything in the Bible was becoming more real to me. As we read the Gospels, Jesus became something more than an historic figure. He was vivid and present, and He was speaking to me. I found myself being drawn into the stories of the Gospels. I felt as if I were tagging along with the disciples on the dusty roads of Palestine. I felt their movement, their conversation, their amazement at the Lord's sayings and works. This entered even into my sleep so that when I dreamed, I would often see a clear picture of Jesus leading His band of disciples along the bank of the Jordan River. In those dreams I would find myself looking at them from the opposite bank. Then Jesus would slowly turn around and look at me, and the disciples also, shielding their eyes with their hands against the brightness of the sun. One night when this took place, Jesus turned again and He said to me, "Why don't you cross over and join us?" And so I splashed through the water and came into their company. It was on the next day that I received, during a time of quiet meditation, my clear call to the ministry. I have always felt that God had channeled this through the devotional study of the Bible.

If this leaves the suggestion that God only uses the Scripture in this way to call people to the ministry, I have been misinterpreted. He has a living word for every person, in every walk of life, for everyday involvements. I recall a young businessman who was almost dragged to one of our prayer groups by another young man who had found fulfillment in this fellowship. I could sense the young businessman's discomfort. It was not difficult to tell how he felt when you saw him sitting on the edge of his chair with his eye on the door, his escape hatch. As we got into our informal Bible study he relaxed a little, and finally he settled back in his chair and became very thoughtful, his eyes becoming more and more alert. He seemingly could not contain himself any longer, and he said with amazement, "They're talking about me and my life." It was the beginning of a new way of living for him as he became a truly dedicated layman, alive with Christ.

One of the great advantages of Bible meditation is that it is possible to enter into the scriptural sequences with "stop-action." Sometimes, in home movies, we want to stop and look at some particular picture, so we backtrack, stop at a selected scene and simply concentrate on it for a while before moving on. It is very advantageous to be able to do this with the Bible. In a way, we have an opportunity which the disciples themselves did not have. Things kept moving on as they followed Jesus and sometimes they could not absorb the meaning of one encounter before they found themselves in the midst of another. We can stop the movement at any point and ask, "What is this saying? What does this mean to my life? Why did this point of action stand out for me like a bright light?" Then we can absorb ourselves in that suspension of time until the significance becomes clear to us.

The discussion of this step of meditation melds naturally into the next.

6. **Receive.** In the process of meditation, pray that you might be able to perceive what particular word God has for you today. This step distinguishes itself from the former in a significant way. In the last step you were entering into a scriptural passage. You were open to whatever God might be saying to you. In this step you are focusing more directly upon a specific direction for your life as it is being experienced today. In other words, you are working from the general to the particular.

The former step would be like the disciples who were at the feeding of the four thousand. They saw it, they experienced it, they were involved in it. But a short time later they were not ready for the next step as Jesus quizzed them about the significance of that event for their thinking, for their growing relationship with Him. "Why do you discuss the fact that you have no bread? Do you not yet perceive or understand? Are your hearts hardened?" (Mk. 8:17). Then Jesus reminded them of the feeding of the five thousand and of the twelve baskets that were taken up. If they had been more perceptive, they could have understood that He was revealing to them His messianic mission to gather up the twelve tribes of Israel. Then he reminded them of the feeding of the four thousand and of the seven baskets which were taken up. Again, if they had been more spiritually perceptive, they would have understood that He was the Savior of the world who had come to gather up the seven symbolic gentile nations. But they did not yet understand. It had everything to do with their apostolic commission.

In this step, then, not only do we see ourselves in the biblical scene with Christ but we perceive the meaning of that event for our relationship with Him and the application to our particular lives. Jesus does not deal with us in the abstract but in the concrete. This leads us to the next step.

7. **Relate.** Having received a particular word for our life as it is lived today, we are called upon to relate it positively in terms of an actual response. It is possible to have received and clearly understood what Christ is saying to us but then to fail to agree to do anything about it. That is the significance of this step; to say "yes" to God. We have entered meditation in vain if we do not have an agreeing spirit. How often we get to this point of discovery and begin objecting! This is where the "but, Lord" comes in. We realize that this is not the direction we had wished for, and so we hedge. We hope that perhaps the Lord might reconsider and give us multiple choice.

We need, then, to flash back to that stage of meditation where we had submitted ourselves to God in reliance and trust. He does not reveal a way for our lives which does not stem from love, love for us and love for others. If it means some form of self-offering, it is the service of perfect freedom. Here is the strength of Mary's response, "Behold, I am the handmaid of the Lord; let it be to me according to your word" (Lk. 1:38).

8. **Remember.** One cannot enter quiet meditation without remembering the needs of others. It becomes quite natural to enter into a time of intercession when we have become more acutely sensitized by the presence of our Lord to the lives of those around us. Meditation, in some popularized versions, seems to lead people to more exclusiveness, more concern with one's own feelings, and self-fulfilment. Christian meditation, however, leads us to look outside ourselves. This is

because we become more consciously a part of the Praying Church; we are of a wider fellowship. It does not lead us to a hermitlike existence but to a Christ-like compassion for more and more of His creation.

Intercession is our greatest act of love for others. We can do no better for others than to lift them into Christ's presence. We are not left with the false alternative, which has often been set up by critics of prayer: the choice between "prayer" and "action." Prayer *is* action, God's action. Again, it does not leave us removed from the subject of our prayer, for we have offered to give whatever might be required of ourselves if God can use us in any way in the answer to that prayer.

Intercession can be a very exciting enterprise for the Praying Church. How vivid is the memory of that day when I received a telephone call just after dawn. It was the anxious voice of one of my parishioners (call him Ned). His wife (call her Laura), who was not yet forty, had just had a paralyzing stroke. He had called the doctor, and an ambulance was on the way to pick her up. His very next thought was to have the prayer chain notified. This was a network of intercessors who could be called within a few minutes. Over fifty were involved. The prayer chain was activated right away and I quickly drove to the hospital. I arrived at the emergency entrance at the same moment as the ambulance. There I saw Laura being taken out on a stretcher. Ned was with her. I went up to Laura as they began wheeling her in the door. It was pitiful to see this young person, with her familiar friendly face, unable to move or speak. She could only express herself with her eyes which were bright and hopeful in spite of her condition.

As soon as she was settled in her hospital room, I went in with Ned. We prayed together, even as we knew that more than fifty others were praying all around the city. I laid hands upon her and left. It was Good Friday and I was to preach the Seven Last Words of Christ in a three-hour service in a downtown church. During that service my prayers of intercession kept going out for her. They seemed particularly pointed as I meditated upon the suffering of Christ. Yes, He knows the meaning of human suffering.

As soon as that service was over I returned to the hospital. I was met by a smiling Ned who quickly ushered me into Laura's room. She was sitting up in bed, dressed in a bed jacket, with a radiant smile on her face. Not only that, but she greeted me with her voice. She had perfect diction! It only took her a moment to tell me, with tears of gratitude to God, that all her paralysis had left her. She could walk! In the past hours, heads of staff from the hospital had rushed in to see her because they could not believe what they had heard about her. They unabashedly referred to her as "the miracle girl." After a few days of observation she was back home perfectly well.

Imagine Easter Sunday with this family! In church Ned and all their children were seated near the front row with beaming faces. Surrounding them, at various points of the church were all those people who had prayed in the intercession for Laura. They too were beaming. The resurrection of Jesus Christ took on powerful meaning as the obvious evidence of His risen life was being proclaimed in this act of healing. It was a healing of far greater than physical dimension, for the knowledge of the presence of the Lord in the Praying Church reverberated to all the Body of Christ in that place. Nor would it be contained there, for the exuberance of these Easter people was to be felt in many places as it radiated outward.

9. **Rededicate.** Each time of quiet meditation is also an opportunity for rededication of our lives to Christ. Every honest Christian will agree that, though we have been called to His kingdom, we are apt to walk in and out of it several times in a day. We may surmise that this was St. Paul's

reason for saying that he must die to that residue of the old pre-Christian, sub-Christian self which still rears up its ugly head. Thus, before any day passes, we dare not lose the opportunity of rededicating ourselves anew to Him and His Kingdom. We may have wandered from Him during the course of the past twenty-four hours, but now we know that we must declare our love and loyalty to Him once more. It is a simple act, like re-establishing a relationship with a friend whom we may have ignored as if he did not exist. We may not have deliberately set out to hurt him, but we have been so insensitive that we were completely tuned out of his feelings, his personhood.

So it is in our rededication to Christ. We declare again our love for Him in the quiet of meditation. It is not a frantic expression but a calm declaration; one that simply enjoys Him for Himself and not for any desire of need-fulfilment. Here again, I often find myself saying the Jesus Prayer.

10. **Renew.** A final step in this way of meditation is that of renewal. Certainly we find ourselves renewed in the very process. But be constantly reminded that it is not the act of meditating itself that renews us but the presence of Christ within that act.

Inevitably we are led to the fellowship of other Christians when we have met Christ in meditation. We want to be with others who know Him. This is where the greatest acts of renewal happen. We do not remain in meditation of this kind forever. (This is not to say that we do not, in another living sense, pray without ceasing.) This, again, differentiates Christian meditation from some popularized forms in which people have become so imbued in the meditative process that it has become an end in itself. They find themselves more and more withdrawn from the world, from people. I know of one case in which a person was engaged in a non-Christian form of meditation to the extent that she would lie upon the basement floor looking up at the rafters all day long. This, in spite of the fact that she had several children to care for. She finally realized that she was becoming unbalanced when she encountered a Christian fellowship which taught her a new and living way. Christ does not take away the dimensions of life but expands them.

Thus we find ourselves being led into a rhythm of life which involves us in quiet prayer as we live in the Scattered Church, and which brings us back again to the praise and worship of the Gathered Church. There we find the corporate ways of renewal which Christ has provided: the fellowship of those who are bound together by the same Spirit, the sacramental life by which He extends His grace, the call to muster in His army.

14 Prayer in the Church Triumphant

In the beginning of this book, as we began to look at the Praying Church, there were chapters on "Prayer in the Gathered Church," "Prayer in the Apostolic Group," and "Prayer in the Scattered Church." There is yet one part of the Church which is to be considered—the Church Triumphant. This is the Church in the Great Day of the Lord. It involves us in eschatological teachings, the promises of His Coming in the Second Advent. What does prayer mean in relationship to the Church Triumphant? What effect does the thought of this have upon our present prayer life?

Many of the so-called mainline churches have difficulty in speaking of this matter. It becomes a source of embarrassment to them. It is a subject which seems dearer to the hearts of many of the smaller revivalistic churches. It is quite possible that some of the aforementioned embarrassment stems from the zealousness of the more demonstrative of these groups. Many churchmen are wary of becoming associated with the teachings of those who, accompanied by a flood of tongue-in-cheek newspaper publicity, have declared that the Lord would return on such and such a day on a hilltop near Los Angeles. The day was prepared for with great excitement as the adherents sold or gave away their property and began camping out on top of the hill as the time drew nigh. Then the hour would come and pass and nothing would happen. The crowd would finally gather themselves up and wander disconsolately to whatever place they could now find in their severed ties with the world. Such occurrences become a stumbling block to a serious consideration of the eschaton.

However, it is still there. The clear teachings of Jesus in the Gospels and the Acts of the Apostles cannot be erased from the record. It is as distinct as any other of His teachings. If one were to pick and choose among His promises, or from the stories of His activities, when one part or the other is unpalatable to us for one prejudicial reason or another, we should have created a whole new field of Bible interpretation. It would be interpretation by personal taste rather than by the process of exegesis, which allows the entire unexpurgated text to speak for itself.

We must deal with it, and there is no reason why we should do it reluctantly. The understanding of the full round of God's plan is needful for a prayer life that is based upon total reality. A prayer life that does not see God's ultimate plan for the Church would be seriously short-circuited. It could be likened to the bee that hovers around one blossom while failing to see the fields of blooms that lie beyond. If all we can contemplate upon are the things of this world, our view of God's plan would be no less short-sighted.

It is not nearly so difficult to deal with the Second Coming if we simply pay attention to the clear words of Christ on this subject. He told us that it is not for us to forecast the future. The future is in God's hands, not ours. He made it very plain that no man could know the time of His Second Coming. He said, "But of that day and hour no one knows, not even the angels of heaven, nor the Son, but the Father only" (Mt. 24:36).

What He wanted us to hear was the message that we

should *always* be ready for His coming. "Therefore you also must be ready; for the Son of man is coming at an hour you do not expect" (Mt. 24:44). This was not meant in a sense of foreboding as many have taken it. Why should one who is alive with Christ be afraid of His coming? We don't need to know the time of that return as long as we are in a constant state of readiness and glad anticipation. This is what ongoing prayer is. We are joyful to have Him near; we could not be anything but overjoyed to have Him nearer.

When I was a child, I had a recurring dream which I now feel was given to me by God as a cosmic framework for a life of communion with Him. It was a dream that took all morbidity out of thoughts of Christ's return and made it a day of greatest victory. It was a dream I started having when I was only six years old. For years afterward the same dream would occur in exactly the same way; not one single detail was different from the time before. In that rare phenomenon in which one maintains a conscious realization that one is dreaming on a level apart from the dream itself I would find myself thinking, "Here it comes again!" Then it would unwind almost as if it were on a reel to be projected over again.

I was walking up a dirt road leading into the village where I was born and raised. The road came in from the east. On the right of the road there was a slope thick with trees, the houses being barely visible through them. The weeping willows hung over the road. The branches were waving in a light breeze and the birds were gaily singing. On my left there were rolling fields ripe with grain. Only a short time ago did I realize the symbolic significance of the fields ripe for harvest. Ahead of me lay the village itself. Since the sun was setting, it appeared mostly as the dark silhouette of trees. Above it, starkly outlined, was the steeple of the church. Suddenly everything grew awesomely still, as it sometimes does before a refreshing summer rain. The trees on my right ceased moving and the birds stopped singing. There were no signs of traffic or movement anywhere. However, the fields on my left seemed to be melting into a multicolored sea. The waving of the grain became, as it were, undulating waves of rainbow colors. Ahead of me the sun was below the horizon. I stopped still in my tracks to see what would happen next, for the air was prickling with anticipation. Then, out of the setting sun a new sun began to rise, brighter than any I had ever seen, and the thin clouds above the horizon were illuminated in glorious color. Then I heard the sound of a trumpet. I knew in my heart of hearts what was about to happen! The Lord God was about to proclaim His Great Day! Then I would awaken. Each time I would awaken just before the Lord was to speak. I never woke up frightened but always comforted. I had a great feeling of God's loving presence. I had a comfortable picture of a God who had all things in His hands. He had a grand plan that was beyond this temporary isle, and those who had a grip upon His timeless life had nothing to fear, only the joy of anticipation.

This has meant everything to my prayer life since that time. I find myself praying within the context of the total scheme of God. I am able to see the world as His beloved creation, but I am able to see beyond its time to the eternal realm. The Praying Church needs to pray within the scope of eternity. We can see time as a line which has a beginning and an ending. This line is surrounded by the unending ellipse of eternity. Even as we live upon this line there is no point above, below, behind, or before which is not penetrated by eternity. It touches each point of the time line and passes through it. To be a Praying Church within that vision is to understand the meaning of our Lord's saying, "And this *is* eternal life, that they know thee the only true God, and Jesus Christ whom thou hast sent" (Jn. 17:3).

The Praying Church also recognizes that the true evaluation of this world is one which recognizes the impermanence of this world. Here we have no abiding city, but we seek one that is to come, beyond history and beyond death. Our final citizenship is in heaven. The utopian is a ghastly pessimist: to think of life going on and on into a far distant future, ruthlessly sacrificing the toiling, sorrowing, dying, generations of humanity to eternal oblivion, so that the last and luckiest generation may reach the earthly paradise before they too go down into the darkness of annihilation—this is the heartless pessimism of the utopian dreamer.

The beginning of the End has already been realized in Christ. If any man is in Christ, there is the New Creation, the Age to Come; he has tasted of its powers. For Christ, all old things are passed away; all things thenceforward are new. In Christ, the Eternal Now, the Eternal Yes has been given to our experience. Our Christian life in time is the foretaste of an eternal order of blessedness in God. The age to come is a present experience but also a future consummation. We still have to die; but death changes its meaning when a man knows he has already tasted of the life beyond its portals. Only that end of life makes sense of all that we do, all that we strive to do. It gives the setting for all our prayers.

Such a teaching does not invite a relaxation of our efforts for the good of man and this world. It actually encourages creative, loving action because it gives meaning to all existence, temporal and eternal. We know that our labor is not in vain in the Lord, therefore we can be steadfast, always abounding in His work (1 Cor. 15:58). If we love here, we shall love the more there. If we create here, we shall create the more there. If we fight the good fight here, victory will be eternal in scope. If we worship God here, we will commune with Him in His house there. If we live with Him in the fellowship of prayer now, we will have the fellowship of the Holy Spirit in the Communion of the Saints there.

I can remember a time in which I considered myself more sophisticated about these matters. I was particularly amazed, and somewhat amused, that the people of Thessalonica could have been so naïve as to expect the return of the Lord in their own lifetime. I thought that they must have been quite simpleminded and childish to have such expectations. Didn't they have any sense of ongoing history? It seemed that St. Paul dealt with them rather gently in counseling them to keep on with their work, and assuring them that if the Day of the Lord did not come within their own lifetime, the dead would be the first to be gathered up to meet Him.

Now I see them in a different light. They were not naïve. They were charged with hope and expectation regarding His coming. He filled their thoughts and prayers so completely that they could yearn for nothing greater than to see Him and to be with Him forever. Could there be a better yearning? It must have been with tearstained cheeks that early Christians heard the last words of the New Testament, " 'Surely I am coming soon.' Amen. Come, Lord Jesus! The grace of the Lord Jesus be with all the saints. Amen!" (Rev. 22:-20–21).

Even now the waves of time are lapping up on the shores of eternity and none of us knows when the last wave will come in. But when it does we shall be on the eternal shore praising Him. Our prayers will be answered. The Praying Church will be the Church Triumphant.

15 The Praying Church

"And when He drew near and saw the city He wept over it" (Lk. 19:41). It was Palm Sunday. After the triumphant passage over the Mount of Olives where the shouts of "Hosanna" were still ringing over the hills, the sight of a weeping Christ might have seemed incongruous. Yet if they had known what the next five days would bring they might have wept with Him. These thoughts must have been in the mind of Jesus as He paused to look at Jerusalem, and they became focused as His eyes swept over the sight of the walls and towers of the Holy City. Ordinary men might have seen solid structures defying the forces of destruction, but Jesus saw beyond and within them. He saw a city of people—corrupt, troubled, evil, prepared to kill their Lord. Jerusalem was a microcosm of the world of humanity He had made. He wept for all people.

Then He said, "Would that even today you knew the things that make for peace!" Having entered the city, He immediately headed for the temple to pray. Some would have said that, if He was so concerned about the city that He would weep over it, He ought to have engaged in some social reconstruction project at this point. But instead He went to the temple to pray because He knew the things that really belonged to the peace of the city of Jerusalem. The corruption would not be truly and profoundly overcome by new projects and programs because the same unchanged and corrupt people would administer them. Peace and change would only come about by changed people—people who would know the peace of God which passes understanding.

Then, when Jesus came to the temple he declared, "It is written, 'My house shall be a house of prayer.' " The house of God is the house of *prayer!* It was in God's presence, by communion with Him, that change would come and peace would reign. So it was that when He came to the house of prayer, He found it to be, instead, a place of merchandising and no little swindling of the poor, a den of robbers. It was a place so confusing and out of tune with God that no one could be still there before His presence. There were even those who scurried through it as a shortcut from one part of the city to another.

So He began to cleanse the city at its heart, its place of prayer. Recall again what He said, "My house shall be called the house of prayer." The house of God is the house of prayer. How plainly Christ speaks! There is no confusion or pretentiousness. In recent years it was quite a popular practice for conferences to be held to discuss the question, "What is the purpose of the parish church?" The question was good and it needed to be asked, but, unfortunately, many leaders of such conferences left the impression that there was no real answer to that question, and, as a result, the conferees went home in a whirling mass of confusion. Undoubtedly, the intention of the conference was some kind of cleansing of the temple. The buzz groups left the people buzzing for a while, but when all was said and done much had been said but little had been done.

Impressions had been left that the parish church exists for any number of reasons—for community service, political agitating, cultural preservation, social activity, education, the benefit of its members, organizational work, pastoral functions, group dialogues. Most of these sound quite wholesome and important, but they could also be very ambiguous and exhausting.

Then consider again the simplicity of Jesus' words (Yes, now we are unashamedly harping upon it), "My house is the house of prayer." The house of God is for communication with God! It is where we meet Him in adoration, confession, thanksgiving, intercession, and petition. It is where we come in praise and stillness before Him. It is where we break bread with Him at His table, an act of holy communication.

Something so vital is being said by our Lord. He is saying: "Begin and end everything in me. Do nothing without my will and blessing. Do everything by my might and inspiration. This is my Church. I will tell you what to do with it. This is my world; I will tell you what my design for it is. You, individually, are mine. I will reveal my plan for your life. Above all, worship in my house is not only a means to an end; it is an end in itself. It is the one experience in this life which you can be sure will endure into the next life."

Does all this mean that a parish church has no other work to do? Of course not. There are many, many directions for local church life: service to the community, youth work, Christian education, evangelism, our individual callings seven days a week, and a hundred other things. However, unless they begin in prayer and continue by His blessing, they are not His work. Unless we fall on our knees, all that we attempt to do will fall on its face. We are committed to no other work than His, but this encompasses all creation, all this world and beyond to the next.

Those who consider prayer a cop-out, a place for hiding, do not know what real prayer is. It is a place where you come out of hiding and expose yourself to Christ. It is a place of surrender where God asks, "Who will go for me?" and your answer is, "Send me." Yes, Jesus wept for the city of Jerusalem because they had forgotten the house of God, the house of prayer. Thus it was God Himself they had forgotten. Without Him they could do nothing for the city of man. If anyone in our time weeps for the city of man, let him first come into the house of God, with the fellowship of the Body of Christ, to be cleansed, renewed, filled with His Spirit, and sent forth in His name and in His strength.

Let this be a modern parable of the Praying Church: When I was in charge of a congregation in Duluth, one of the magnificent views was that of the sparkling expanse of Lake Superior, the great inland sea. How often I would go near the lake and see ships and boats of every size and description plying its waters and disappearing over the horizon. At times, in spite of the rough waters, I would see people in rowboats.

In this parable, a group of people, men, women, and children, are out rowing in the middle of Lake Superior. There is a great storm. The wind is very strong and the waves are very high. They are straining at the oars. Their backs are weary; their hands are blistered. They are determined, however, to reach the safety of the shore. If they give up, they will be swamped with water and sunk, going down to an icy death. If they manage to stay afloat, they will be dashed to pieces on the jagged rocks of the shore. But as soon as they rest they are swept back to the place where they started. This goes on for what seems like an interminable span of time.

Then, someone notices a bundle in the front of the boat. It is a sail! They must have wondered why that wooden pole was standing up in the middle of the boat. They set it up and quickly hoist the sail. Just as quickly they begin to head for the safety of the port, effortlessly, quietly, powerfully. The power is not in their hands; it is in the wind! All they needed to do was to hoist the sail up into it. Yes, there was work to do—to use the chart and compass they had been given, to steer a steady course. But now they could make it. The journey would not be exhausting but exhilarating.

The parable need not be spelled out, for the Praying Church knows its meaning. He who has ears to hear let him hear. One only has to remember the description of the Day of Pentecost when the pioneers of the Church waited for the power to do His work: "And suddenly there came a sound from heaven as of a rushing mighty wind."

Study Guide
for *The Praying Church*

This guide is designed to be used individually or in small groups. The questions pertain to the material found in each chapter of *The Praying Church.* They are intended to bring out the teaching of that chapter and also to help individuals or groups to explore their own experience of prayer.

A group or individual is advised to use no more than one set of questions at one session. In some cases it may be desirable to spend two sessions on one chapter. As "hurry" is not the ideal for prayer neither is it in the study of prayer.

A leader should be designated in a group setting. This role could be reassigned from week to week. The leader's role is to:

1. Begin the discussion and keep it rolling.

2. Portray a style of warmth and straightforwardness, never threatening or pompous.

3. Be ready to give illustrations out of his or her own life.

4. Encourage all persons to take part. It sometimes helps to ask someone a question like, "How does that sound to you?" or "Does this remind of anything in your life?"

5. Be alert to persons who would monopolize the dis-

cussion. If anyone is argumentive ask them if they would hold their thoughts until the group is done and have a private discussion with you.

6. Keep the discussion on the level of personal experience, the concrete rather than the abstract. The purpose is not academic but that of personal and group growth in Christian spirituality.

Since the study is centered on prayer try to spend some time in prayer. It's one thing to talk *about* God and prayer; it's another thing to speak *with* God in prayer.

Chapter 1: Prayer in the Gathered Church

1. Describe some specific occasions when the act of worship had a great significance for you.

2. What are the elements of worship which are most moving to you?

3. What does it mean to "love God for Himself"? What does this have to do with worship?

4. What brings people to a Sunday service? How does one weigh the relative motives behind "desire" and "discipline"?

5. What are your expectations of worship?

6. What do you believe that your role is in worship?

7. What difference does it make if you come as a praying person?

Chapter 2: Prayer in the Apostolic Group

1. What are some of the characteristics of a healthy prayer group? What are some of the unhealthy ones?

2. Design a "format" for a one-hour prayer group session. Compare yours with others.

3. What did our Lord mean when he said, "Wherever two or three are gathered together in my name there am I in the midst of them"?

4. How can we ensure that Christ will be the leader of a group?

5. Why did men who traveled such distances to tell of their prayer life find their small-group experience so rewarding?

6. How would you go about creating a prayer group in your parish or neighborhood?

7. What does it mean to have a "prayer partner"?

8. How can every church organization be involved in prayer (vestry, board, choir, youth group, church school, etc.)? What difference would it make?

9. How would you go about family prayer?

Chapter 3: Prayer in the Scattered Church

1. Discuss the thought of being a member of the Church when you are "on your own."

2. Have you ever "bargained" with God in your personal prayers? Think about it and discuss it with others in the group.

3. What is the prayer of relinquishment? What is it that we hold onto?

4. Identify a particular circumstance or time when you made a significant step forward in your prayer life.

5. What is the difference between saying to God, "if it be your will" and "according to your will"?

6. What "signals" do you get that it is time for some earnest praying?

7. What is the difference between conscious and unconscious prayer?

8. Have you experienced "the recapitulation of Christ's life" in your own in any way?

9. What does it mean to pray with expectation? What is the difference between expectation and fantasy?

Chapter 4: Being and Praying

1. Discuss our Lord's saying, "Love your neighbor as yourself." How can you love your self without being selfish?

2. What does it mean to "affirm" the people around you? Think of ways of doing this.

3. Why is your prayer life so tied in with your image of yourself?

4. There is an old saying, "Pride goeth before a fall." How does this fit in with one portion of this chapter? Can you relate some experiences along this line?

5. If Christ loves you as you are, what does this suggest concerning your attitude toward others?

6. What prevents Christ's gracious acceptance of us from becoming a matter of smug self-satisfaction?

7. What happens to your prayer life when you are depressed?

8. What happens to your prayer life when you are egotistic?

Chapter 5: Dealing with Our Voices

1. Discuss the relationship between thinking and praying.

2. How do you deal with that "voice" within you that tells you what is expedient, what you ought to be doing?

3. How do you deal with that part of you that speaks to you of your physical needs, desires, and drives?

4. How do you deal with that deep-within voice that speaks of ultimate longings of the spirit?

5. People often speak of "hearing" God when they pray. How do you hear Him speaking to you?

6. Think of some of the ways God spoke to people in biblical times. Do you know of any parallels to these in modern times?

7. Discuss some of the words in our Christian vocabulary such as "communion," "community," "fellowship," "communication," "relationships." How are they related to prayer?

8. What is the meaning of "submissive listening" in our prayer life?

Chapter 6: Prayer in a Scientific Age

1. Tell of any encounters you have had with people of the world of science, both those who denied faith and those who affirmed faith.

3. How do you respond to people who deny the possibility of answered prayer?

3. Have you ever experienced what you believe to be a miracle? Have you had difficulty sharing it with others? Would you share it with this group?

4. Discuss your own conflicts between what you consider to be natural law and the intervention of God.

5. Many have pointed out that many doctors have less difficulty in believing in prayers for healing than people who are not associated with medicine. How could this be true?

6. Discuss the author's statement, "What we call a 'miracle' from our standpoint as human beings is simply a 'mercy' from God's side."

7. Discuss the author's statement that scientists are now discovering "that religion is not needed for the unknown as much as it is needed for the known."

8. Discuss ways that living daily in a secular world effects the level of expectation in our prayer lives. How do we counteract this?

Chapter 7: Prayer and the Human Factor

1. Do you believe that intercessory prayer can actually be effectual over great distances? Can you give examples from your own experience?

2. How have you been able to deal with the problem of a finite human being reaching out to an infinite God? What if someone tells you, "You don't have to speak to Him because He knows everything anyhow."

3. What point is the author making when he says that much of what is taken as "unanswered prayer" is "rejected prayer"?

4. How do you handle your intercessory prayer list: length of list, how long people are kept on it, how often you pray, what is the nature of the prayer?

5. Why is the concept of the Praying Church so important when we consider the imperfection of our personal prayers? Discuss the difference between "praying to Christ" and "praying with Christ."

6. Why do you think that God included prayer in His plan for humanity? What does it say about the nature of God?

7. Discuss the whole question of prayer in relationship to the gift of freedom.

8. How does praying for others, and for situations, affect your own life?

Chapter 8: Prayer in the Valley

1. Try this experiment with others in your group. Let each person bend a piece of flexible wire into the contours of the moods and experiences of the past month. Compare these and, if it is not embarrassing, discuss any hills or valleys that developed.

2. Discuss the author's reference to these reactions to the valley of suffering, namely, wailing and stoicism. Have you reacted in these or in other ways?

3. How do you pray your way through the "valley of guilt"? How do people deal with guilt if they do not bring it to God?

4. Have you ever gone through the dark night of the soul? If you have how did you come out of it?

5. What are the dangers of expecting our spiritual life

to be based upon our feelings? Can a plateau be as beneficial as a mountaintop experience?

6. How do you pray about the reality of death in the midst of life? How does your attitude about death affect your daily life? Discuss some personal experiences with death and how your relationship to God was affected.

Chapter 9: Prayer as God's Commission

1. When you have heard the expression "renewal" what did you think it pertained to?

2. What are some of the negative things which come to your mind when you hear the term "relevance"? What positive things?

3. What things have been introduced in your parish as ways of renewal? How have parishioners reacted to them? Has renewal come?

4. What am I doing about my own renewal? Are there any new elements in my spiritual life? Has my way of praying changed in the past year or so? Share this with others in the group.

5. Discuss the author's statement, "A renewed Church is a praying Church." What happens otherwise?

6. Refresh yourself on the story of E. Stanley Jones and the fruit tree. Does this speak to some of the frenetic activity of our daily lives? Does it mean we would become passive?

7. Discuss the author's reference to Jesus "walking through his ministry." What does this say to us?

8. What evidence of the renewal of prayer do you see in the Church? How can this renewal be enhanced?

Chapter 10: How to Succeed in Prayer

1. How familiar to you are the responses to prayer mentioned at the beginning of the chapter: (a) those who don't pray and don't want to; (b) those who pray but only to themselves; (c) those who want to pray but don't know how to begin; (d) those who have lapses in prayer?

2. What is meant by "success" in prayer?

3. How would you respond to people who are afraid that much prayer would lead to fanaticism?

4. How would you respond to people who express the thought that prayer is a form of escapism?

5. How do we know that prayer is ordained by God (and is therefore given validity)?

6. Discuss the prayer life of Jesus Christ. What does it suggest to us?

7. Have you had hang-ups about praying out loud or extemporaneously? If so why?

8. Discuss prayer in terms of straight forward conversation with God.

Chapter 11: Giving Yourself with Your Prayer

1. What does it mean to "let God have your life" in reference to prayer?

2. What have you found it necessary to relinquish in order to have a more effective relationship with God?

3. Why are we often reluctant to accept God's will completely?

4. Discuss Jesus' saying, "For their sake I consecrate myself," within the context of John 17.

5. Can you tell of any experiences in which you were led to offering yourself along with your prayer (or the experiences of others)?

6. Take some moments of quiet and see if you can think of roadblocks to prayer because of something you feel unable to offer to God. Discuss the Christian rhythm of "emptying" and "filling."

Chapter 12: Quiet Prayer

1. How do you react to quiet and aloneness? What is the "sound level" of your own home or place of work?

2. Discuss the relationship of spiritual health to the hectic pace of life in which most people are involved.

3. How will you find a space or place for quiet in this kind of world?

4. Discuss the story of the man who broke down and said, "There must be something more?" Can you relate to this feeling?

5. When you have dealt with external noise how do you deal with "internal noise" that remains? Discuss means you have used to relax before prayer.

6. How do you react to prayers such as the Jesus Prayer as ways of focusing attention upon God? Can you distinguish between "vain repetitions" and wholesome repetitions. What ways have you used for focusing your attention on God?

7. In speaking of relying upon God distinguish between the meaning of "faith" as belief and its meaning as trust.

8. Share experience you have had in which you have learned lessons about reliance or trust.

Chapter 13: From Read to Renew

1. Discuss how your group have used reading in devotional life.

2. How do you use the Bible for meditation? How can

God's gift of imagination be used with this kind of meditation?

3. Select some narrative from the New Testament and let each member of the group meditate upon it in silence. Share your discoveries.

4. What does it mean to say "yes" to what God reveals to you? How do you test the validity of what you hear to be God's will for you?

5. What is meant by the statement, "prayer is action"?

6. What particularly impressed you about the story of the woman who suffered a stroke?

7. How, within the context of The Praying Church, do you make sure that mediation does not become a personal "trip"?

8. Review the steps of meditation by going through all of them in an act of quiet prayer that takes no less than thirty minutes.

Chapter 14: Prayer in the Church Triumphant

1. Out of your own background of understanding how have you thought of "the end of the world"? Compare this with the understanding of others in the group.

2. What does it mean to pray within the context of this expectation? How can we be both in the world and not of the world?

3. Review our Lord's teachings on the subject of His ultimate return. Where are they found in the Gospels? Read some of these passages aloud and discuss them.

4. How does your prayer life keep the discussion of Christ's return from becoming morbid or unattached to daily life?

5. Have you ever thought of the existence of the Church in terms other than those of this world? How does this

thought fit in with the analogy of the Church as the Body of Christ?

Chapter 15: The Praying Church

1. Share with others the part of this book which was most helpful to you.

2. Discuss the purpose of the parish church in terms of inculcating the spiritual life. How does this branch out into other functions of the Church?

3. What happens to these functions if there is no prayer? Can you give examples of "wheel-spinning" activities in the Church which have lost their meaning?

4. How do you feel that prayer can be related to (a) evangelism, (b) youth work, (c) community outreach? Think of other functions of the Church and how prayer enters in.

5. Discuss the parable of the sailboat. What does this have to say about the effectuality of the Church locally, nationally, and worldwide?

6. Where does the work of the Holy Spirity begin?

7. What does it mean "to pray without ceasing"? Share ways in which you have tried to keep your attention upon God in all times and places.

8. Have you made any decisions as a result of this study? What are they? What action do you plan to take?

9. Write out a rule of daily prayer which you feel would be realistic for you. Compare this with others in the group.

10. Discuss this statement by a prominent world churchman when asked where the Church would be most alive fifty years from now: "That will be where the people of prayer will be found," he said.